A HIMALAYAN HOPE
AND A HIMALAYAN PROMISE

India's Spiritual Vision of the Origin, Journey,

& Destination of Earth's Environment & Humanity

Thomas E. Pliske, Ph.D.

PACEM IN TERRIS PRESS

Devoted to the global vision of Saint John XXIII,
author of the famous encyclical letter "Pacem in Terris"
and prophetic founder of Postmodern Catholic Social Teaching,
and devoted to the search for a healing Postmodern Ecological Civilization
that will draw on the rich spiritual and philosophical wisdom-traditions
of our entire global human family.
(www.paceminterrispress.com)

Pacem in Terris Press publishes scholarly books directly or indirectly related to
Catholic Social Teaching and its commitment to justice, peace, ecology, and spirituality,
and on behalf of the search for a Postmodern Ecological Civilization.

In addition, to support ecumenical and interfaith dialogue,
as well as dialogue with other spiritual seekers,
Pacem in Terris Press publishes scholarly books from other Christian perspectives,
from other religious perspectives, and from perspectives of other spiritual seekers
who promote justice, peace, ecology, and spirituality,
for our global human family and for our wider family of all creatures.

Opinions or claims expressed in publications from Pacem in Terris Press
represent the opinions and claims of the authors and do not necessarily represent
the official position of Pacem in Terris Press, the Pacem in Terris Ecological Initiative,
Pax Romana / Catholic Movement for Intellectual & Cultural Affairs - USA
or its officers, directors, members, and staff.

PACEM IN TERRIS PRESS
is the publishing service of
the Pacem in Terris Ecological Initiative,
which is the core project of

PAX ROMANA
CATHOLIC MOVEMENT FOR INTELLECTUAL & CULTURAL AFFAIRS
USA
1025 Connecticut Avenue NW, Suite 1000,
Washington DC 20036
(www.paceminterris.net)

ABOUT THE AUTHOR

THOMAS PLISKE is author of many scientific articles on ecology and entomology, and of the memoir LIGHT, TRUTH AND NATURE: *Reflections on Vedic Wisdom & Heart-Centered Meditation in Seeking a Spiritual Basis for Nature, Science, Evolution, and Ourselves* (Pacem in Terris, 2016).

He received a B.A. in Biology from Amherst College in 1963 and earned his PhD in Evolutionary Biology from Cornell University in 1968. He is also Environmental Adviser for Science & Vedic Spirituality for the Spirituality & Sustainability Global Network.

He has taught courses in deep ecology, sustainability, ecology of south Florida, epistemology, environmental education, spirituality and sustainability and study abroad in Costa Rica. He is currently Lecturer Emeritus in the Department of Earth and Environment and adjunct faculty in Religious Studies at Florida International University in Miami.

He lives in Miami with his wife Drishti, an Ayurvedic medical counsellor. Both are regional coordinators for the *Sri Chinmoy Oneness-Home Peace Run*. Since the early 1970's, they have maintained a spiritual center which serves the south Florida area by teaching free classes in meditation skills.

TABLE OF CONTENTS

Photo by Martin Jernberg

India is not just a place. India is not just a people.
India is the celestial music, and inside that music
anybody from any corner of the globe
can find the real significance of life.

Sri Chinmoy. 1997.
INDIA, MY INDIA – MOTHER INDIA'S SUMMIT-PRIDES.
(Agni Press, Jamaica, NY. p. 15.)

1

PREFACE &

ACKNOWLEDGEMENTS

When Everest climbers depart base camp, they have hope and determination that they will arrive at their summit-destination and that the destination will fulfill their aspirations. This book contains a map for the ascent and illumination of human consciousness that was drawn millennia ago. It offers the assurance of wise, seasoned climbers who journeyed successfully and stood upon the peaks towering high above our world. Their message is that the Promise of the Destination is real and is reaching out to guide and inspire us even before we glimpse the shining heights on the horizon.

> *The heart-meditation lives at top of the Himalayas.* [i-1] *As soon as one sees the Himalayas, one is reminded of his own inner divine qualities, peace, light and bliss in boundless measure as well as his outer qualities, concern, patience, compassion and dedication.* [i-2]

This book is dedicated to Sri Chinmoy, my guide and teacher of nearly five decades, and who has personally experienced all the inner human capacities discussed in its pages.

I am grateful to the Sri Chinmoy Centre and the Sri Aurobindo Ashram Trust and Publication Department for permission to quote from Sri Chinmoy's and Sri Aurobindo's writings respectively.

Many other people deserve thanks for their contributions and inspiration to the realization of this book. Special gratitude goes to my patient and wise wife, Drishti Pliske and to the indefatigable encouragement and technical help of Prof. Joe Holland of Pacem in Terris Press. Many thanks also go to Alo Devi Siddha, Elisabetta Ferrero, Begabati Lennihan, Sumadhur Alan Page, Alan McManus, Vajra Henderson, Martha Keys, Mindahi Crecencio Bastida Munoz, and *Roshi* Philip Kapleau.

INTRODUCTION

We are grateful to God, for He is with us here and now. We are Grateful to God, for He has created within us a genuine hunger for Him. We are grateful to God, for He has given us a long express-train of hope. We are grateful to God, for He has repeatedly told us that He will keep His Promise. What is His Promise? His Promise is that He will not be satisfied unless and until each creation of His satisfies Him in His own Way. [i-3]

W e live in a time when currents of fear, hopelessness, oppression, division, anger and anxiety swirl past us at every moment. We want our lives to assuage and heal our world plagued as it is with poverty, violence, injustice and escalating heart-breaking environmental destruction and pollution. Yet, even as we experience an apparent widespread submersion of goodness, kindness, happiness and justice, we are simultaneously aware of a higher more illumining standard, an innate "moral compass" within ourselves and within the world. That compass tells us that we have much more in common than differences that divide us.

Nearly all of us cherish memories of acts of compassion, love, charity and courage often long after the experiences themselves have passed. These memories give us happiness, inspiration and a measure of hope. Numerous points of light and joy are still shining in our midst, but since the spotlights of attention tend to accentuate the shadows, they do not always receive the recognition and gratitude they deserve. Still, we have an inner sense that knows hope and the promise of a more fulfilling path, ascending, progressive and trans-formative, leading to a world where sharing, harmony and happiness are the norms.

This book is a brief exploration of India's spiritual wisdom from its ancient genesis in Vedic times to its place in the 21st century, par-ticularly as a framework for integrating the dynamics of our personal lives with those of the Earth and with universal Nature, the cosmos. It is a system perhaps unrivalled in its inclusiveness and detail, that can help us find, follow. and ascend that path of hope, promise and fruitful deeds.

The idea for the project germinated over dinner with my long-time friend and colleague Joe Holland, Professor emeritus of Philosophy & Religion at St. Thomas University. We were both participants in a conference on Spirituality and Sustainability in Assisi, Italy, in June 2018, and were discussing whether there was any concise but com-prehensive text that connected Indian spirituality to the deepening environmental crises of our times. I conceded that I felt there was nothing of the sort, but that I would give it serious thought. This book is a fruit of that thought.

As I began to imagine how the manuscript could take form with-out running into many hundreds or thousands of pages, it became clear that it could not take the form of a comparative religious, ethical or philosophical study. Nor could it explore and review all the phil-osophical ramifications of Vedic wisdom, because, like science, the Indian spirituality bases itself on expanding empirical evidence, hands-on, soul-on *experience,* of *yogis* who have entered and claimed spiritual Truth as their own.

My intent is to present the major aspects of Indian spiritual wis-dom and plead the case why it is vitally important and useful for navigating the waters of our own times. There is an already enor-mous and growing body of writing and tradition, from every corner of the human cultural landscape, that is relevant and connected to the

Indian tradition. To steer a course between writing a cumbersome text and embracing the greater clarity that accompanies brevity, I have elected to cite only a few of these important works in the text and append a longer and more inclusive list of references at the end of these chapters, which readers can consult according to their personal interest and needs.

The terms *yoga* and *yogi* have become so much a part of popular culture, especially in the arena of commercial hatha yoga and fitness, that the terms need clarification. Yoga in these discussions pertains to the spiritual disciplines which an individual undertakes with the goal of uniting his personal consciousness with the Divine, the universal consciousness. A *yogi* is one who has achieved this union, a fully realized soul, or one whose progress places him on the brink of achieving this goal. A *rishi* is a seer of Truth through whom the wisdom of the Vedas is revealed.

Accordingly, it is with the flag of *experience* atop the mainmast that we must chart a course. I hope readers will forgive the necessity of waiting to bring in most of the environmental issues until the final chapter, because there are many contingencies that need to be on the table before we can have the full context of that discussion.

My account I hope will not only be informative but also practical and practicable to readers. Articles of faith, from whatever source they spring, find their true value, meaning, expression and practical value in the lives of their practitioners. India has produced a vast depth and breadth of experience, which is open to everyone who is asking questions about their individual identity, purpose and connections to our planet home and to the universe, and how they can engage in transforming themselves and the world.

Evolving humanity is at a crossroads where we are experiencing a tug-of-war between *clinging and daring* – clinging to our baser divisive and possessive tribal nature, our fears, attachments, anxieties and doubts, and daring first to imagine and then invoke, claim and embody the higher consciousness in which we all share and in which we are all enjoined. If we are daring and determined, then it is possible to participate in creating a world where peace, harmony, trust, sharing, gratitude and beauty are values that are communally established, prized and nurtured.

As we struggle in the "battlefield of life" [i-4] our innate spirituality is compelling us to aspire and discover in the depths of our hearts the true meaning and fulfillment of what it is to be a member of the human species. It is asking us to dare to reinvent and rewrite our own personal stories, expand our identity and in the process redefine our self-image and our relationship to the Earth and the cosmos. Once achieved, that discovery cannot remain cloistered but needs translation into radiant deeds that reveal and manifest that Truth at the foundation of our personal lives and of the world. We are crying for the certainty that we can make a difference, to have the assurance that we can face many daunting challenges arrayed before us. Spiritual Truth requires of us courage, both for self-discovery and for action.

The ancient practitioners of the Vedic tradition and their modern representatives reveal that spirituality is innate in man as part of the universal creation, regardless of any religious, cultural, racial, social or economic affiliation. Spirituality does not exclude, cancel or invalidate anything. It simply embraces and adds illumination, just as turning on the light illuminates the objects in a dark room and reveals their relationships to one another.

The eminent Jesuit theologian Pierre Teilhard de Chardin [i-5] is reputed to have remarked, *"We are not human beings having spiritual experiences, but spiritual beings having human experiences."* What the Indian *rishis* discovered, and what we discover in spiritual practice, is the highest in ourselves, an inner existence, joy and capacity beyond any intellectual knowledge, wealth, power, or skills that we may cherish or have already attained. Accordingly, the name they gave to anything that binds us to a lower, limited, finite existence is *ignorance,* a quality we all share in some measure until full realization dawns.

That all in the created universe, including everything that we think inanimate, is spiritually alive and connected, is the most basic truth of *yoga* and of most other great spiritual traditions of the world, especially indigenous traditions. Put another way, everything in the universe has consciousness, although it may be of a very limited nature.

Millennia before Darwin or the dawn of astrophysics, *yogis* understood that the entire cosmos was evolving. They arrived at this conclusion not by the objective study of physical Nature but from immersing their individual consciousness in an oceanic inner oneness with the cosmic deities and universal Nature. Their application of evolutionary law to humanity originated from their inner empirical spiritual experiences.

The fact that this ancient flowering of spirituality began in India as many as 20,000 [i-6] years ago does not diminish its value today in the 21st century. The *rishis* never considered the Truth they experienced to be their own possession or the possession of the kingdoms or cultures of their time. As pioneer explorer-seers, they were the first to bring into and anchor in terrestrial existence a high universal Essence of which all humankind is not only the beneficiary but also its vessels.

Later masters – for example, Krishna, Christ, Shankara, Chaitanya, Gautama Buddha, Troilanga Swami and Lahiri Mahasaya – while adapting their teachings to their own disciples in their own societies, regarded themselves as strong, inseparable and all-encompassing branches of the same tree of realization that nourished their self-realized progenitors. Each master regarded the supreme Truth as One, available to whomever had the aspiration and determination to become its instrument, and each master developed and expressed his realization in a new, expanded and unique way without compromising the integrity of the Truth he realized.

If we are realistic in our view of the world, it is our unavoidable conclusion that our species has suffered cycles of divisive sectarianism, struggles for power and possessions, aggression, and destructive conflict throughout most of its history. Yet, it is also true that we are evolving. Expansion of scientific understanding now holds planet Earth as part of a cosmic unity; and the advent of peaceful, cooperative global organizations such as the United Nations give us markers to chart our progress.

Our times are generating a frisson in the human psyche. There is a thrust pushing us to progress, but a prelude to that progress requires us to envision what kind of world we want to inhabit. What kinds of relations between humans and the Earth, between one human group and another and between humans and their Creator are the goal of our aspirations? Embedded in the choice is the necessary mustering of our inner will to move our vision in the right direction. From within there is an inexorable prodding to enlarge our receptivity, inclusiveness of mind, our ethics, to exercise a measure of inner discrimination and courage to find the paths upward and forward. As C.S. Lewis wisely reminds us, *"We can't go back and change the beginning, but we can start where we are and change the ending."*

Since their inception, all human cultures have relied upon their spiritual and religious traditions to understand their existence and to interpret and respond to their interactions with one another, with the natural environment and with the unknown forces and worlds that move beyond the spheres of their ken. Nearly always, certain individuals who have probed deeper into themselves or universal Nature, who have travelled within the spiritual worlds and have gained their wisdom, have served as masters, gurus, shamans, teachers and guides for their brothers and sisters who have not yet attained their vision but have faith in their inspiration and experience.

Like all traditions, the Vedic scriptures and teachings have two distinct aspects that need to be recognized and discriminated.

- First, the ancient *rishis* who personally experienced the highest truths of the universe – passing them on orally to their disciples or to the kings whom they counselled – did so in the language and context of the prevailing cultures and societies. Therefore, many of the rituals and poetic images taking their origins in the local familiarities of that time are not applicable to our times, or they need sifting for their symbolic or mythic import.

- Second, and most significantly, there are the eternal Truths that the knowledge imparts which are applicable to all men, in all times and all cultures. It is to this latter category that we must pay greatest attention.

A summary of the major features of Indian spirituality includes the following, all of which I will discuss in detail in later chapters.

1. Creator and creation are one Being guided by a Supreme Will, a unified consciousness throughout, whether or not we might consider any part of the universal existence as living or inanimate, spirit or matter, good or evil, thought or deed, silence or sound, exoteric or occult. The Creator has compassion for every aspect of creation without exception.

2. In humanity, the development of mind (rationality) allows the consciousness either to remain tied to our superficial physical surroundings or to transcend that limited scope and awareness and enter into higher realms of existence and purpose.

3. The creation is synonymous with its evolution. Spirit has become involved in matter, and it is in the process of evolving inexorably toward the Light from which it originated.

4. Human spiritual progress, the progress of souls, individual and collective, whether slow and unconscious or expedited through spiritual disciplines or by a realized master, is coterminous with a simultaneous self- and world-transformation.

5. There is an integral environmental and evolutionary continuity of the terrestrial creation in time. Birth, death, and reincarnation

assure the retention of progress made by souls and its continuity in the next embodied life. Like a river, the net evolutionary movement of our world is always forward and upward by the gravity of the Creator's Will. Although, to our minds, there are periods of apparent regression, both human hope and divine Promise are inextinguishable.

6. Human action and thought obey the Law of Karma. Under most circumstances, what one does has a reflexive effect upon the doer, who is responsible for his actions. The effect may be rapid or delayed by one or more incarnations. The Law applies specifically to humanity and not to any part of the physical environment, plants, or animals.

7. In the process of rebirth, the soul incarnates first in the mineral aspect of earth, then in plants and animals before entering human existence. Once the soul takes human form, it acquires the capacity of self-awareness and does not revert to animal life. Eventually, after many human incarnations, the soul realizes the Highest in itself and thereafter does not again incarnate physically unless so instructed by the Creator.

8. The higher and inner planes of awareness to which humanity has access are the domain of many levels of beings from those close to our physical reality to those of exalted position and glorious presence (e.g. angels, archangels, cosmic gods and goddesses)

9. All aspects of creation embody three primary qualities (*gunas*) in various admixtures of expression: darkness, avoidance and inertia (*tamas*), dynamic movement, craving and excitement (*rajas*) and illumination (*sattva*). In the evolutionary-transformational process, there is gradual movement from *tamas* to *sattva*, but in the highest levels of spiritual realization, one transcends the three *gunas*.

10. Spirituality, consciousness, and life are properties of the universal creation in *all its forms* and are not confined to any human race, culture, religion or group.

11. Indian spirituality accepts the world and humanity as they are now, full of egoism, cruelty, aggression, greed, violence, ignorance and death, with the view to their assured eventual transformation.

12. The purpose of life is to realize and embody the highest Truth, the Truth of the Creator. Fully realized souls are no longer bound by the forces of terrestrial Nature, but they become ego-free instruments of the divine Will, at one with the universal consciousness.

13. Fully realized *avatars* or masters i-7 periodically appear on Earth to inspire, serve and guide humanity. This is especially true during times when the forces of ignorance become very powerful and threaten to obstruct evolutionary progress.

Before proceeding further, I need to make some distinction between spirituality and religion, although for some this line of thought is probably not possible or fruitful. The Vedic traditions have given rise to the religions of ancient Vedism, modern Hinduism, Buddhism, Jainism and Sikhism to name a few of their larger derivatives. Numerous masters of high caliber have contributed both to the pure spirituality and to the religious variety and depth of the Indian subcontinent, and countless other sages have added their wisdom to building up complex systems of philosophical thought i-8 based upon them.

Religion (e.g. Judaism, Hinduism, Islam, indigenous shamanic traditions) implies a specific and more or less exclusive ritualistic pathway to Truth. The word's Latin meaning is literally to "bind back" (*re* + *ligare*) or reconnect (*sic:* to Truth, Source, the gods). Spiritual Truth is the ineffable *experience* that underlies all religions that are predicated acknowledging a benevolent Force higher than ourselves and transcendent to our intellectual, rational conceptions. It is an inner radiance and joy of being that draws seekers to great, realized souls and stimulates the religious forms by which the masters' followers try to bring balm to their struggling societies. Throughout the following chapters, I have endeavored to emphasize the value of the *experiences* of great spiritual figures rather than any specific religious doctrine.

Many seekers today classify themselves as "non-religious" truth-seekers or God-lovers, indicating that they embrace no specific religion, or have created a practice assembled from many sources that fits their particular needs. The inner dimensions of Truth that the *rishis* discovered in ancient India are resources to be used, part or parcel, of all sincere seeking, whether religiously-based or not. It is important that the reader understands that the Peace, Light and Delight that both the ancient and modern masters contacted and brought forward from deep within their consciousness is innate in everyone, even if a given individual is not aware of it or rejects the idea altogether. It is a Truth alive and well in every human soul on Earth today and indeed in every aspect of the cosmic creation. It is ours to experience and claim as our own.

Very few realized spiritual masters have had the capacity or inclination to write about their inner experiences as a part of their service to the world and to their students. I have selected two, whose lives were closely connected, both of whom wrote voluminously. Both were fully acquainted with the challenges of the 20th and 21st centuries. They are windows through which we can glimpse the clarity and vastness of their world views as they relate to our own lives and institutions. Accordingly, the majority of the citations in my book are direct quotations from their writings.

Sri Chinmoy (1931-2007) was born in Bengal (now Bangladesh), and spent 20 years immersed in intense spiritual practice at the Sri Aurobindo Ashram in Pondicherry, India. In 1964, he came to New York City to share his inner wealth with sincere seekers, remaining there until his passing. Today, he serves as a spiritual guide to disciples of diverse ethnic and religious backgrounds in numerous centers worldwide. He advocates the "Path of the Heart" rather than a path of the mind. All his teachings advise us to open our hearts and directly experience and cultivate the qualities of divine, selfless love, oneness, self-giving and acceptance. He saw this as the simplest way to approach the Supreme consciousness within and to make rapid spiritual progress. In the classic Vedic tradition, Sri Chinmoy taught that God and man are aspects of the same unified consciousness. Man attains fulfillment by realizing that God is none other than his own highest self, and God reveals Himself through man, who in turn serves as an instrument for world-transformation and perfection.

Sri Aurobindo (1872-1950) was born in Kolkata, India, but from the age of seven was educated in England, culminating in studies at Cambridge University. Upon his return to India in 1893, he worked as a college professor in the Princely State of Baroda. In 1906, he resigned his university post and became an editor of the newspaper *Bande Mataram* i-9 to take up the cause of Indian nationalism. He was arrested and detained three times for championing India's independence from Britain, and in 1910 he moved to Pondicherry in what was then French India.

There he withdrew from politics and concentrated on intense yogic practices begun earlier in Baroda. Making rapid progress, he achieved full realization and began to formulate a new spiritual path, *Integral Yoga*, in which the goal was personal and world-transformation through the power of the *supramental consciousness* i-10. In 1926, in cooperation with his spiritual collaborator, The Mother, he founded the Sri Aurobindo Ashram, which accepts not only Indians but also seekers from diverse nations and spiritual backgrounds.

In the early 1940s, after the death of his parents, Sri Chinmoy moved to the ashram along with his three brothers and three sisters. There in his early teens he attained the experience of full realization. Though living in the ashram along with hundreds of Sri Aurobindo's students, he played the role of a normal active and intelligent young disciple. Keeping his powers well concealed by his humble and quiet demeanor, he existed unrecognized by most of his fellow ashramites. However, Sri Aurobindo and The Mother *did* recognize his spiritual development. They provided a nurturing and loving environment in the ashram for Sri Chinmoy to prepare and strengthen his inner life until he was ready to depart for the United States in 1964. [i-11]

Although the same powerful spiritual current flows through the teachings of both masters, Sri Chinmoy adapted his path and spiritual guidance to Western seekers, most of whom had little or no understanding of Indian culture, spiritual traditions or spiritual masters. Rather than remaining aloof and secluded from his students he was friendly and approachable, holding frequent meetings, answering thousands of questions, identifying himself inwardly with their individual problems and level of spiritual development in order to facilitate their inner growth. He gave public programs and concerts both in the United States and abroad, visiting more than 70 nations over the 43 years of his sojourn in the West.

In keeping with his "Path of the Heart", he transmitted his experiences in writing primarily through tens of thousands of brief, profoundly mystical aphorisms and poems. At the time of his passing he had completed more than 50,000 in a projected series of poems, entitled *Seventy-Seven Thousand Service Trees.* Even his lectures and essays have a mantric, lyrical, intimate and poetic quality. His primary goal is to awaken the hearts rather than challenge the minds of seekers. In addition to literary capacity, he also composed thousands of songs in both his native Bengali and in English. He told his students that soulfully sung spiritual songs (akin to the traditions of Indian *kirtan* and *bhajan*) [i-12] could be even more powerful than meditation in elevating the consciousness.

In addition, he developed a style of spiritual painting and drawing that he called *Jharna-Kala* (Fountain Art). Over a period of more than 40 years he created tens of thousands of spiritually evocative paintings, as well as more than 10,000,000 drawings of birds, which he saw as the representatives of human souls.

Although he was also a poet, Sri Aurobindo expressed his realization with greatest puissance and radiance through the penetrating

14

precision and enlightened intellectual clarity of his prose. His writings cover nearly every aspect of human enquiry and endeavor making him a natural bridge between the realm of spirituality and the fields of religious studies, philosophy, science, social dynamics and creative arts. His most widely read works include *The Life Divine, The Synthesis of Yoga, Letters on Yoga, Essays on the Gita* and *Rebirth and Karma (The Problem of Rebirth)*.

Notes for Preface,
Acknowledgements, & Introduction

i-1.   Sri Chinmoy. 2008. *My Christmas-New Year Vacation Aspiration-Prayers, Part 59.* p. 66.

i-2.   Sri Chinmoy. 1976. *Aum Magazine,* Vol. II, No. 3. June 27.

i-3.   Sri Chinmoy. 1987. *Everest Aspiration,* p. 98. Agni Press, Jamaica, NY.

i-4.   *The battlefield of life* is the constant struggle between the divine forces and undivine (*asuric*) forces within us. If we aspire for a higher truth, then the divine (*sattvic*) forces will gain victory; but if we take the side of our desires and lower nature then the undivine forces will continue to dominate us. This is the essence of the *Bhagavad Gita,* one of India's most sacred scriptures. In the Gita, a dialogue takes place between Arjuna, his army's greatest archer and his guru, Krishna, a fully realized yogi and also Arjuna's chariot driver. Arjuna has thrown down his weapons and refuses to fight against the asuric forces of the Kaurava clan, which includes many of his relatives. Arjuna's dilemma can be resolved only when he surrenders to the highest Will   within and allows Krishna to guide his actions in battle.

i-5:   Pere Pierre Teilhard de Chardin (1882-1955) was a distinguished French Jesuit priest, theologian and philosopher. Having obtained a doctoral degree in geology with a specialization in paleontology, he combined Darwinian evolutionary theory with aspects of Catholic doctrine to produce a novel cosmology that united matter, life, mind and spirit. He envisioned the apotheosis of the creation to be an *Omega Point* in which creation and Creator are united in Christ-Light. The details of his mystical synthesis he expounded in his major writings: *The Phenomenon of Man*, *The Future of Man* and *The Divine Milieu*. The spiritual basis of his evolutionary vision of man has remarkable parallels to the Vedic tradition. Contemporary geo-theologian Thomas Berry was significantly influenced by Teilhard de Chardin's thought.

i-6: The astrological basis of measuring duration of ages of the Earth and human history (*kalpas, yugas, sandhis*) set forth in the *Vishnu Purana* and other sacred scriptures, produces significant differences from Western historical and scientific estimates. The same system of astrological dating also maps the upward spiral evolutionary track of humanity and the ebb and flow of consciousness that characterizes it. For a fuller explanation, consult [Swami Sri Yukteswar. 1974. *Kaivalya Darsanam: The Holy Science*. xxiv + 77 pp. Self-Realization Fellowship, Los Angeles, CA.]

i-7. In his writings, Sri Chinmoy makes detailed distinctions between different levels of illumination. These are exhaustively documented in [Sumadhur. 2018. *Sri Chinmoy, fully realized spiritual master, his life and philosophy*. 600 pp. Sumadhur Publications.] In this book, I rely primarily on three terms which appear frequently in the discussions.

1) *illumination* and *illumined* indicating that the person or subject has touched upon the source of spiritual, inner Light or has Light to some degree.

2) *realization* or *fully realized* is a level of yogic attainment in which there is permanent union with the Supreme Will (Sri Chinmoy) or *supramental* consciousness (Sri Aurobindo). Once attained, one never falls back into ordinary awareness. Yogis who have not yet achieved the summit of this transformation may have abundant Light, but you will at times descend to lower levels.

3) the term *avatar* has taken on various meanings and connotations in popular culture. In these discussions, an *avatar* is an incarnation of the Creator Himself who takes human form. In the Indian tradition, two of several examples of avatars are Rama and Krishna. In the fourth chapter of the *Bhagavad Gita*, Krishna tells Arjuna, "*Whenever unrighteousness is in the ascendant and righteousness is in the decline, I body Myself forth. To protect and preserve the virtuous and put an end to the evil-doers, I manifest Myself from age to age.*"

i-8: This book follows the orthodox position, based on Vedic Scriptures. Specifically, this is a *monistic (advaita)* doctrine positing a single Source to Creation and a unified evolutionary process. Some other branches of Indian philosophy take up a heterodoxy in which there are separate spiritual principles governing yogic consciousness and Earth-consciousness. Students who wish to pursue the philosophical fine structure of the orthodox vision can consult Sri Aurobindo's *The Synthesis of Yoga*. 1971. 872 pp. Sri Aurobindo Ashram, Pondicherry, India.

i-9:   *Bande Mataram* is the title of the Indian National Song, written by Bankim Chandra Chatterjee during the struggle for independence from the British (as opposed to the national anthem *Jana Gana Mana*). It was also the title of the eponymous newspaper, begun in 1905, of which Sri Aurobindo became the chief editor and a major contributor. Published in English and strongly promoting Indian nationalism, the paper was distributed throughout India and even quoted frequently in the *London Times*. Both the song and the newspaper are credited as major factors in awakening the people of India to their struggle for independence from Britain. Independence was eventually won on Aug. 15, 1947, coincidentally(!) Sri Aurobindo's birthday.

i-10: The consciousness above and beyond the mind, the Supreme Will guiding the evolution of the cosmos.

i-12. This early phase of Sri Chinmoy's life is discussed in detail in Sumadhur's (2018) study cited in i-7 above.

i-13: Both are centuries-old traditions of Indian devotional singing. *Kirtana* most often are stories told or sung about spiritual personages or from the epics *Mahabharata* and *Ramayana*, accompanied by musicians. *Bhajans* are songs of devotion which may have one or more singers and instrumental accompaniment. Sri Chinmoy wrote many *bhajans* and created a special group of women singers and musicians who perform them worldwide.

1

STANDARDS FOR TRUTH

Asato ma sad gamaya
Tamaso ma jyotir gamaya
Mrtyor mamritam gamaya.

Lead me from the unreal to the Real.
Lead me from darkness to Light.
Lead me from death to Immortality.

Brhadaranyaka Upanishad [1-1]

Yogic wisdom & Truth

If we are going to have faith in the yogic experience of Truth, we necessarily will have to have faith in the yogis themselves. For any of us who have asked the questions "What is Nature?", "Who am I?" or "Why is the world the way it is?" the cumulative Indian spiritual wisdom deserves our most serious consideration, for it is the most detailed map ever made of the inner realms of human consciousness. If one had the time, it might be possible to assemble all the threads of Truth from other spiritual and religious sources, but here they can be had in a single package.

The Vedas of prehistoric India are most likely humankind's earliest spiritual scriptures, and they give significant clues to the origin of the tradition of integral self-knowledge or *yoga (sensu stricto).* (See pp. 6-7).

At the outset, it must be said that the scope and methods of yogic wisdom are not comparable to those of rational-intellectual or scientific knowledge. Neither is yogic truth susceptible to verification by any academic or scientific standards. The latter are incomplete modes of knowing, yet are embraced by the former. Paradoxically, like science, it is empirically based. Its vision comes from a transcendental perspective, beyond any understanding of the detail of the physical universe or Nature and beyond any activity of logic, inference, reasoning, deduction, or extrapolation, beyond mind itself.

The seers of both ancient as well as modern times know that the human species began evolving as an essentially mental being. Although risen out of a lineage of animal Nature, and carrying more than a smattering of animal propensities, humans are charged with a high destiny to evolve beyond the limitations of the *physical mind* [1-2] and the ceaseless desires that emanate from the lower emotional consciousness.

Sri Chinmoy, in his poetic description of the mind, tells us,

O my mind, vast are your responsibilities. You have to please your superiors: heart and soul. Only with your warmest admiration will you be able to conquer the heart. Only with deepest faith will you be able to conquer the soul. You have also to satisfy your subordinates: the body and the vital. [1-3] *Only with your purest concern will you be able to make the body smile. Only with your genuine encouragement will you be able to help the vital run unmistakably toward good and not pleasure.*

O my mind, I need you desperately, either to abide in you or to go beyond you. You see and thus protect the physical [1-4] *in me. You serve and thus reveal the spiritual beyond me.* [1-5]

It is essential to understanding yogic wisdom that we view the mind as an evolving and still imperfect instrument of our consciousness, not as its pinnacle. As Sri Chinmoy implies, the full *sattvic* nature of the mind cannot emerge until mind is surcharged and identified with the higher Light of the spiritual heart and soul. Otherwise, the darker struggling world of cravings and pleasure that makes up the vital and body consciousness, pulls the mind down into that domain. This is the arena of the animal milieu, from which the mind has emerged and from which it is aspiring to ascend.

The mind is a bridge to our higher, illumined capacities. The yogic vision within us is beckoning us to take courage, arise, awake, and climb higher.

Because the spiritual reality generated by the yogic vision is not only universal but intrinsic to human existence, elements of its Truth have surfaced in many times and places. The hopes and goals of its elements are not new. They are present in the sacred teachings of nearly all religions, and students of all disciplines, ranging from sciences through art, music and philosophy, have encountered them, e.g. in Socrates, Aristotle, St. Francis of Assisi, Spinoza, Goethe, Bach, William Blake, Emerson, Whitman and in Darwin's champion, Alfred Russell Wallace. Although enshrined in the annals of human culture, these flashes of transcendent clarity have tended to remain egregious for their cultural environments, or at worst, considered seditious, viz. the fates of Socrates and Christ.

In India, transcendent vision is a firm cultural foundation and a perennially guiding presence. It has survived the epic struggles recounted in the *Ramayana* and *Mahabharata* [1-6] and more recently the occupations of the Moghuls and the British. Inextinguishable, it prompts the thoughts and guides actions of contemporary Indians from the depths of their souls. It does so not by claiming exclusivity or superiority over other life-paradigms, but by embracing them.

As described in this and following chapters, India is placing at humanity's disposal a solid link between the terrestrial and transcendent. This link assures us that we have faculties beyond the outer senses and the physical mind, beyond even the intellectual mind, which interprets and analyzes what the senses convey to our consciousness. The trick is to get the experience of the transcendent and then integrate the much more limited scientific and intellectual perspectives under its umbrella.

Truth-seekers of the Vedic era entered the forests and mountains, not so much from any outward compulsion or desire to escape their responsibilities, but because they had not found satisfaction in their ordinary lives. Loved ones had died, wealth had not brought the hoped-for security or fulfillment, age and infirmity took away or dulled vitality and pleasures of youthfulness, and power brought no peace in its wake. None of the desires and goals of ordinary human life brought the expected happiness. Fear, doubt, frustration, anxiety, anger and insecurity remained, despite ephemeral success and achievement. On the contrary, the new seeker entering an *ashram* depended on inspiration from the light, purity and peace emanating from the established yogis, despite their simple and even austere lifestyle. Novices aspired to gain admittance to this source of bliss and took up the spiritual practices under the guidance of their elders.

The method of instruction, *guru-shikha* (spiritual master-disciple), paired novices with accomplished masters who could guide the experience and practice of the newcomer. Because the guru had established his access to the higher worlds of consciousness and had fully identified himself with his disciple's strengths and weaknesses, he was in a position to prescribe the exact sort of *sadhana* [1-7] to spark the most rapid progress in his disciple. Today, this instructional paradigm remains as the most sacred relationship of Indian culture, based solely on the flowering of the inner nature in the disciple guided by his master. Sri Chinmoy has discussed this relationship in detail in his stories, essays and lectures. [1-8]

In 1998, the Religious Studies Department at Florida International University in Miami invited Sri Chinmoy to receive an award for his work promoting world harmony. The title of his acceptance speech was, *Indian Philosophy, a Glimpse* [1-9]. He prefaced his address by reciting one of his poems written when he was a young man still living at the Sri Aurobindo Ashram.

The Absolute

No mind, no form, I only exist.
Now ceased all will and thought
The final end of nature's dance
I am it whom I have sought.

A realm of Bliss bare, ultimate
Beyond both knower and known.
A rest immense I enjoy at last;
I face the One alone.

I have crossed the secret ways of life,
I have become the Goal.
The Truth immutable is revealed;
I am the way, the God-Soul.

My spirit aware of all the heights,
I am mute in the core of the Sun.
I barter nothing with time and deeds;
My cosmic play is done. [1-10]

He remarked afterward that this poem represents a view transcendent to philosophy and to mind itself, and that the fundamental aspect of Indian philosophy is that it is based on both matter and spirit. It embraces *experiences* of the spiritual heart and soul, not only of those of the outer world as perceived by the senses and physical mind or even by the intellectual subtleties of philosophy. He intended insult neither to intellectuality nor to philosophy as he pointed the way to an expanded realm of human experience and divine actions.

It was not his arrogance that spoke. It was a humble invitation to explore and claim the Truth he offered. Sri Chinmoy's poem projects certainty, strength, and victory, not the voice of one who has any fear, doubt or who has shrunk back from the vastness it communicates. It is the voice of one who has entered that domain and identified with it and claimed it as his own.

Provided we can accept Sri Chinmoy not merely as imaginative, but as a poet-seer (*kavi* is the Sanskrit word for such visionaries), who has had extraordinary experiences of self-discovery, we are led to wonder, what is the true potential of the liberated human spirit, awaiting discovery in the higher realms of consciousness beyond form, desire, thought and expectation.

Although in their time the Vedic communities may have appeared to be unremarkable, indigenous, locally-based spiritual associations, they evolved into something much deeper and more luminous, attaining to a collective empirical wisdom of fully realized souls probably unique in human history. Sri Aurobindo's comments on this phenomenon provide poignant insight,

> *Veda, then, is the creation of an age anterior to our intellectual philosophies. In that original epoch thought proceeded by other methods than those of our logical reasoning, and speech accepted modes of expression which in our modern habits would be inadmissible. The wisest then depended on inner experience and suggestions of the intuitive mind for all knowledge that ranged beyond mankind's ordinary perceptions and daily activities. Their aim was illumination, not logical conviction, their ideal an inspired seer, not the accurate reasoner. Indian tradition has faithfully preserved this account of the origin of the Vedas. The Rishi was not the individual composer of the hymn, but the seer (drashta) of an eternal truth and an impersonal knowledge. The language of the Veda itself is sruti, a rhythm not*

composed by the intellect but heard, a divine Word that came vibrat-
ing out of the Infinite to the audience of the man who had previously
made himself fit for the impersonal knowledge. The (Sanskrit) words
themselves, "drsti" and "sruti", sight and hearing, are Vedic expres-
sions; these and cognate words signify, in the esoteric terminology of
the hymns, revelatory knowledge and the contents of inspiration.[1-11]

Sri Aurobindo in his introduction to the analysis of Vedic culture sums up the early 20th century's grossly mistaken European opinion of the scriptures, one shared as well by many Indian scholars:

The hymns of the Veda are the sacrificial compositions of a primitive
and still barbarous race written around a system of ceremonial and
propitiatory rites, addressed to personified Powers of Nature and re-
plete with a confused mass of half-formed myth and crude astronom-
ical allegories yet in the making. [1-12]

He follows on the heels of this inadequate assessment with a me-
ticulously detailed thesis that quite the opposite is true. In following through his arguments, it becomes clear that the linchpin of his premise lies in his own deep spiritual experiences and consequent capacity to identify with those of the Vedic authors.

Thus there emerged in my mind, revealing itself as it were out of the
ancient verses, a Veda which was throughout the Scripture of a great
and antique religion already equipped with a profound psychological
discipline -- a Scripture not confused in thought or primitive in its
substance, not a medley of heterogeneous or barbarous elements, but
one, complete and self-conscious in its purpose and its purport, veiled
indeed by the cover, sometimes thick, sometimes transparent, of an-
other and material sense, but never losing sight even for a single mo-
ment of its high spiritual aim and tendency. [1-13]

Manuscripts surviving from Vedic times are the four *Vedas* them-
selves: *Rig Veda, Sama Veda, Yajur Veda and Arthava Veda*, comprising more than 20,000 prayers, *mantras* (invocations) and *slokas* (verses). These are addressed to the experiences of the rishis of the Infinite One (*Brahman*) and the various cosmic gods, e.g. Agni (fire), Surya (sun)

and Vayu (air, wind), contacted in the depths of their prayers and meditations. There are also 18 *Puranas* and 108 *Upanishads* based on the Vedic *shastras* (scriptures) but compiled later. The *Arthava Veda* is devoted largely to healing and is the basis of Ayurvedic medicine. The *Vishnu Purana* is concerned with the creation of the earth and humanity. These subjects will be discussed in Chapter 5.

The Role of Nature in Vedic communities

Natural surroundings played a crucial role in the aspirations and practices of rishis in the Vedic era. Sincere Truth-seekers, either singly or banding together in small ashrams, renounced the world of possessions, desires, family, kingdoms, and even intellectual knowledge and entered into the wilderness. There, surrounded by the beauty, majesty and silence of unspoiled Nature, they could give full attention to their *sadhana* where Nature provided the necessities of food, water, shelter, clothing and implements.

Many thousands of years ago, judging mainly by the detailed descriptions of plant and animal life in the epics of the Ramayana and Mahabharata and other early scriptures, dense tropical and subtropical forests covered much of the Indian subcontinent. Along its northern frontier runs the massive Himalayan mountain range where scores of valleys bear rivers that drain southwards into the plains of the piedmont joining the Ganges flowing eventually southeastward into the Bay of Bengal.

These forests and mountains, although much altered by the intervening millennia of human activities still provide a richly charged environment both physically and especially spiritually by offering qualities of, peace, beauty, inspiration, and mental silence in which seekers can focus inwardly. Yogis still live in the Himalayan heights, and the headwaters of the Ganges and other rivers emerging from Himalayan glaciers still are sites of many ancient temples and sacred places.

Cities such Hardwar, Rishikesh and Vrindaban (Benares), nestled at the foot of the Himalayas are home to many spiritual centers and ashrams and are the destination of sacred pilgrimages. To visit these places is to be thrust into an inner environment where prayer and meditation have been practiced for thousands of years. It quickens one's inner life and brings to the fore the awareness of the inner treasures we all house within us.

Science & Yogic Truth

One aspect of inner Truth that the Vedic tradition produced, and which lives today in all branches of Indian philosophy is that there is a single source of existence, *Brahman*, the One without a second. The Creator, the *supramental* (Sri Aurobindo), the Supreme (Sri Chinmoy). *Tao*, the Great Spirit, God, Allah and many names from other traditions reflect the transcendent Highest.

The yogis discovered *Brahman*, not through painstaking observation of outer Nature followed by a series of deductions and extrapolations but by experiencing the Infinite on its own terms and aspiring to enter into it, surrendering themselves unreservedly. What they experienced in their voyages into the ocean of the great unknown consequently fed the ardor of their aspiration to go deeper, higher and further within. They could not use objective language to express their experiences as Charles Darwin did to describe his discoveries of the human and natural communities that he found on the coast of South America during his voyage on *H.M.S. Beagle*.

Yet, poetic glimpses the yogis did record, because only poetry could hint at what they *felt*. In the verses they composed, words and phrases like *Lord of the Flame; Immortality; Universal Life; Omniscient; Brilliant One; The ancient Food; Light pervades all; supreme good; to him who is illumination* and *Larger life* are scattered like diamonds through the mantras and hymns of the Rig Veda. [1-14] In that context, the *slokas* of the Vedas are analogous to the journals and logs that scientists keep to record their objective data.

They started with the Source itself, entire and undivided, and proceeded from there to the characteristics that it manifests in the world as it appears to our physical senses and rationality. They entered into the Light of the Creator that was the creation's Source and became one with the harmony and movement of the Creator's vision. It is from that exalted perspective that they understood their own deepest nature and the true nature of the outer forms of creation.

Western science shares with *yoga* the tool of empirical enquiry. Epistemologically, to see and to experience are to know and to believe. However, science starts with the information generated by the physical senses and physical mind then analyzed by the intellectual mind (data and theory), which at present are taken, with their inherent limitations, as the only credible and reliable source of knowledge about universal Nature. However, science as such cannot say anything about the spiritual forces underlying Nature, the meaning of her evolutionary processes or ultimate destination, because the reverse process of Truth-seeking, moving from the physical minutiae to their Source, is impossible. Therefore, Science simply ignores inner experiences, denies their relevance or sometimes even their existence.

Because Western science and medicine still operate mostly within the self-imposed fence of objectivity, which while useful and necessary to understanding the physical aspects of the universe, they stop far short in a comprehensive account of human existence and experience. In his essay *Materialism*, Sri Aurobindo discusses at length the evolution of scientific enquiry and argues that science had no choice but to *begin* with what can be experienced by the physical and intellectual mind, the world of matter, outer senses and reason, aided by their extensions: microscopes, telescopes, etc.

Materialistic science had the courage to look at this universal truth with level eyes, to accept it calmly as a starting point and to inquire whether it was not after all the whole formula of universal being. Physical science must necessarily to its own first view be materialistic, because so long as it deals with the physical, it has for its own truths to be physical both in its standpoint and its method. 1-15

27

If our sciences, using the spirit of empirical discovery, *continue* by making the leap to accept what Sri Chinmoy terms the "mystic and secret," a vast, new and more encompassing knowledge will dawn. Sri Aurobindo concludes on the same note of progressive optimism:

> *That can be only if we pursue these other sciences too in the same spirit as the physical, with a scrutiny, not only of their obvious and first physical phenomena, but of all the countless untested potentialities of mental and psychic energy, and with a free unlimited experimentation. We shall find out that their ranges of the unknown are immense.* [1-16]

When it comes to the question of proof, yogis take highest Truth-Light as self-evident, the direct experience of the Divine. They do not make or need any attempt at rational proof of their wisdom.

On the other hand, because science relies primarily on the instrumentality of the physical and intellectual mind, any method of proof has to address the imperfections of the primary tools of enquiry. In his many discussions of the human mind, Sri Chinmoy describes the two lowest levels as the physical mind and the intellectual mind. The physical mind by definition remains always enmeshed in the gross physical consciousness. The intellectual mind, while operating in a slightly higher mode is able to operate with abstract and more sophisticated thoughts. However, even the intellectual mind has little or none of the Light native to the soul, spiritual heart or higher levels of mind, while at the same time being subject to the limitations of divisiveness, suspicion, complexity, egotism and confusion (See note 1-2).

In our approach to standards of truth, considering the limitations inherent in perception and thought, we can now understand why such a complex system of verification has developed in secular studies such as natural science. Yet, it seems that, despite these difficulties, our sincere higher nature recognizes the importance of consensus, truthful reporting and of being of service to the world.

Sincere scientists hope that the collection of enough objective data about its subject of study, Nature, and elucidation of the laws and extent of the physical universe will eventually provide a clear, unified understanding of all it contains. It is also fair to say that we hope that in accomplishing this cosmic goal there will be many practical and possibly ethical discoveries that will benefit the world community.

One of the major pillars of sound scientific methodology and proof is the idea of objectivity and its corollary, elimination of bias, i.e. alternative explanations for observed occurrences. These may come from impinging environmental effects or compromising personal motivic influences affecting the observers themselves. The rules for collecting information are designed to sample the full range or dimensions of whatever is being studied and then to analyze the forces affecting and potentially changing it.

For example, an herbal remedy for the symptoms of flu should be tested on more than one or two subjects. The number of subjects should be large enough to include differences in gender, ethnicity, genetics, age and health history. Furthermore, the evaluation of sampling procedures, experiments and statistical evaluation of data, need sufficient scrutiny and rigor to assure the elimination of any financial, cultural, political or religious motives, or the even the attachment of a certain outcome on the part of the researchers, whether positive, to be "right" or negative, to be an iconoclast. Researchers routinely make a sincere effort to identify the major sources of bias, which we take into account in the quest for reliable and acceptable outcomes to scientific research and knowledge.

The process of peer-review is in place to eliminate as much as possible any previously undetected biases or omissions as well as incomplete summary of previous research or logical inconsistencies prior to the publication of results. Publication in "peer-reviewed journals" is a seal of approval for entry into the body of academic and scientific knowledge and truth that will be presented to the rest of the world in books and journals. In the best circumstances of peer-review scrutiny, a double-blind approach is used. Neither reviewer nor author knows one another's identity.

The notions of objectivity and bias, which turn out to be illusory, rest on the implicit assumption that there is a fixed entity, the phenomenon being studied (the object of investigation), different and separate from the subjects (researchers engaged in study). Even if we attempt to confine ourselves only to the parts of universal nature in the immediate environment of the object of study (major sources of bias), it is a hopeless task. The hopelessness derives from four conditions, three of which 21st century science conceives and acknowledges as true about universal Nature.

First, the universe is a continuous and interactive phenomenon in space (the essence of ecological thought and theory), all parts of which are in motion. We at best identify what might be "major" biases and can only guess or speculate about the minor biases. Second, we now see universal Nature in a state of progressive evolution. Trying to "freeze-frame" the truth of anything in a constantly changing flow of events in time is a denial of that process. It is perhaps justifiable to say that, if we restrict the scope of our studies to very small temporal or spatial areas of Nature, we will be less likely led astray by the multitudes of converging forces whose relationships are constantly changing.

Science itself evolves, as does everything else in the physical universe. The history of science is a history of changing and expanding paradigms of our understanding of Nature. Thomas Kuhn [1-17] has analyzed the phenomenon in terms of "scientific revolutions" in which certain receptive individuals, e.g. da Vinci, Copernicus, Newton, Darwin and Einstein pioneer wider vistas of scientific understanding. The revolutionary paradigms are usually rejected at first but eventually accepted as "normal" science. From the spiritual point of view of Sri Aurobindo and Sri Chinmoy, these breakthroughs are part of the will of the Creator driving human progress, manifested by more advanced souls using higher faculties of mind.

A third issue is that with rapid technological development, the rate of discovery of new detail and new relationships within the biological and physical aspects of universal Nature has accelerated rapidly in the past few decades. In 1960, a basic biology text in a college course might have averaged about 400 pages, but today is closer to 1200. Things get out of date quickly, and many scientific texts come out in new editions nearly every year. While some theories remain in place despite the changing factual landscape, in some cases theories too need to be amended or even discarded.

The fourth condition arises from the consciousness of the scientists themselves. All contemporary science is circumscribed by the capacities of the physical senses and the analytical and interpretive skills of the intellectual mind. The product is an elegant comprehension of the external aspect of universal Nature. The domain of the inner aspect lies beyond the pale of any current enquiry. Lest anyone take undue umbrage at this statement, I cheerfully include myself and my ecological research under the canopy of this shortcoming.

Simply put, we are on a journey toward enlightenment and perfection. Sincere, self-giving and sound science, while far from perfect, is part of that journey. A seeker-scientist will only gain more illumination to enter deeper into the wisdom and truth of universal Nature or anything else he studies. Does this mean that we should regard the concepts and benefits of scientific enterprise as unreliable because they are incomplete? Far from it. Once again, we have to remind ourselves that real spirituality never negates anything; it only expands, purifies, illumines and transforms.

Ethical Issues in Science

While contemporary science may be confounded at the highest level by limitations inherent in its mode of enquiry and by the general level of consciousness of humanity, including scientists themselves, the motivational basis of sound science has some ineluctable spiritual qualities. These operate in us despite any agenda of intellect, pride or financial gain simply because we are children of universal Nature, of

Mother Earth. We are no less connected to her than any child is to its mother. There is the bond of indissoluble love at work within us, simply because we are part of the Creation. The magnetism of her vastness, mystery, and beauty to a greater or lesser extent eclipses any shallower theoretical quest for pure information or theory. I have explored these inner motives of science in other essays [1-18]. They are relevant here because they impart, perhaps unconsciously for many people, the intrinsic ethical basis of sound, sincere science.

These intrinsic ethics express themselves in various ways. First, there is the joy that accompanies the expansion of mind into vaster and more spiritual domains. Second and closely linked, is the search for an underlying unity for the physical universe. There is, of course, the reality of the inner oneness, that yogis apprehend as the basis of universal existence, which now is being expressed in the cumulative vision of secular science [1-19]. Third, some scientists, too few in my opinion, are imbued with the view that their art should be of dedicated service to humanity and to Mother Earth, with a collateral *caveat* to be aware of those pathways that could play directly into the hands of the destructive and unscrupulous. *The Earth Charter*, the *United Nations Millennium Goals* and *Sustainable Development Goals*, *The Universal Declaration of Human Rights* and the global environmental movements are exemplary reflectors of this level of scientific ethics.

On the darker side, the ethical challenge of the supremacy and profit motives is a growing pressure, stemming from the increasing financial support for scientific and technological research and development by global military agencies and by private corporations. It follows that there will be expectation of gain or superiority, a motive for producing specific results and for suppressing evidence that might be perceived as harmful to humans, the environment, or the bottom line.

In recent decades, the specter of political influence has affected the credibility of even sound scientific data. This can usually be traced back to the ubiquitous profit motives of corporate industries or individuals who perceive a threat from widely accepted scientific concepts, e.g. global climate change, sustainable development, and the effects of industrial and agricultural pollution on public health and the environment.

Special interests, some based on economic interest and others on conservative religious agendas, have attempted to debase "offending" well-researched facts and their implications by denying or marginalizing them or hiring their own scientists who are willing to stress incomplete, narrow or deliberately biased versions of accepted scientific truths. Some have gone so far as to publish textbooks based on these muddied ideas with the idea of creating public confusion and doubt about sincere scientific concerns and findings.

Indian spirituality finds its source of ethics in the Light of the Divine within us acting in and through the soul and the spiritual heart. In the course of spiritual evolution, soul and heart gradually and inexorably pull the mind toward a more *sattvic*, inclusive identity and higher ethics. Mind must eventually fail to find satisfaction in the pursuits of the physical and vital attraction when it ascends above the clouds of ignorance and desire that shroud the ordinary life. When this transformation begins, it will be heralded by loftier feelings that will include peace, joy, love for humanity and the world and a desire to be of service.

Both Sri Chinmoy and Sri Aurobindo insist that science as it now stands is largely if not completely ignorant of the true nature of the forces that drive what we call Nature and life. Sri Aurobindo tells us frankly:

We shall perceive that until the possibilities of mind and spirit are better known, we cannot yet pronounce the last all-encompassing formula of universal existence. Very early in this process the materialistic circle will be seen opening up on all its sides until it rapidly breaks up and disappears. Adhering still to the essential rigorous method of science, though not to its purely physical instrumentation,

*scrutinizing, experimenting, holding nothing established which can-
not be scrupulously and universally verified, we shall still arrive at
supra-physical certitudes. There are other means, there are greater
approaches, but this line of access too can lead to the one universal
truth.* [1-20]

and

*If indeed all action of life and mind could be reduced, as it was once
hoped, to none but material, qualitative and mechanical, to mathe-
matical, physiological and chemical terms, the opening (in the self-
immuring limitations of materialism) would have ceased to be an out-
let; it would be choked. That attempt has failed and there is no sign
of its ever being successful. Only a limited range of the phenomena
of life and mind could be satisfied by a purely bio-physical, psycho-
physical or bio-psychical explanation, even if more could be dealt
with by these data, they still would have accounted for only one side
of their mystery, the lower end. Life and Mind, like the Vedic Agni
[1-21], have their two extremities hidden in secrecy, and we should have
by this way have hold of only the tail-end: the head would still be
mystic and secret. To know more we must have studied not only the
actual or possible effects of body and matter on mind and life, but we
must explore all the possible action of mind too on life and body; that
opens undreamed vistas.* [1-22]

Sri Aurobindo reminds us that the relationship of spirit to science
is not to dismiss or negate the integrated model of universal Nature
that science has so painstakingly established. Assembling this model
has been an enormous accomplishment of the human mind, bringing
together physical, chemical, biological, ecological, and evolutionary
principles. It is truly a "symphony of a thousand", like Mahler's
Eighth Symphony. Spirituality's task is to lend the grand frame to en-
compass the connections between the physical principles of life and
the higher forces that purposefully shape and guide them.

The ethics that are beginning to emerge from the spiritualization
of science are of a higher and more inclusive order, based on service

to all humanity and the Earth. Twenty-first century technology and scientific enquiry have a wide spectrum of impact on our lives ranging from interplanetary to subatomic and from personal enjoyment and satisfaction to global human and environmental well-being.

Our ethics are not peripheral and sometimes inconvenient theoretical baggage attached to our scientific enterprise. They are statements about the quality of the world we choose to inhabit and how we view ourselves as participants in the universe we are exploring. Our ethics also reveal what we mean by two terms we so often use in evaluating the results of our endeavors, *profit* and *progress*. The ethicist hastens to add - *profit for whom? Progress toward what and for whom?*

Clearly, those who know both the promise and the darkness that currently abide within the practice of science and who know also both the promise and the ignorance within human nature, have the obligation to teach their colleagues and students the numinous ethics of that practice. During the past half-century there have been a number of proposals and discussions about requiring a Hippocratic-style Oath [1-23] for scientists when they complete their scientific education. Most suggest such an oath that would be primarily based on the guideline of Hippocrates, *primo noli nocere* (First, do no harm) but should include a variety of specific positive aspirations as well.

Chance or Guidance?

Another aspect of scientific evolutionary thought is that chance (good luck!) plays a major role in the progressive unfolding of cosmic events. Sri Aurobindo again gives us a higher perspective, including intimations about how we might view the popular aspect of "alternate realities"

Chance, that shadow of an infinite possibility, must be banished from the dictionary of our perceptions; for of chance we can make nothing, because it is nothing. Chance does not at all exist; it is only a word by which we cover and excuse our own ignorance. Science excludes

it from the actual process of physical law; everything there is deter-
mined by fixed cause and relation. But when it comes to ask why
these relations exist and not others, why a particular cause is allied
to a particular effect, it finds that it knows nothing whatever about
the matter.

Every actualized possibility supposes a number of other possibilities
that have not actualized but conceivably might have, and it is con-
venient then to say that Chance or at most a dominant probability
determines all actual happening, the chance of evolution, the stum-
blings of a groping inconscient energy which somehow finds out
some good enough way and fixes itself into a repetition of the process.
If inconscience can do the works of intelligence, it may not be impos-
sible that chaotic Chance can create a universe of law! [1-24]

Sri Chinmoy goes further than an epistemological evaluation. He
has bluntly told us that science, guided by the current lower human
propensities of the vital and intellectual consciousness, has produced
not merely some incomplete but also destructive results. This he has
expressed in his deceptively simple book of aphoristic poetry, *Science
and Nature*: Some examples are,

Science is Power-supremacy. Nature is Love-intimacy.
Science admires division. Therefore, it has division-adversaries.
Nature loves oneness. Therefore, she has oneness-fulness.
Science says to Nature: "To me, you are utterly useless!"
Nature says to Science: "To me, you are deplorably harmful!"
Science is the mind's warship. Nature is the heart's worship. [1-25]

On a more hopeful note, he encourages us:

The human mind has achieved extraordinary marvels; the scientific
mind is the proof. The scientific mind in the beginning was confused,
but now it seems to be going in the right direction and if it really and
truly enters into the spiritual mind, then the success of mankind will
be beyond measure. Now the Hour of God has come. Some of the sci-
entists in the West do believe in God or believe in something they call
'even higher than God.' Wonderful, as long as they feel that there is

some conscious Force or Power in the universe! So, when science sees, in the material world, the possibility of some inner truth, then it can easily enter into that truth and understand that Truth.

Now the Hour has come. Evolution, both the inner and the outer, has come to the stage where people have developed the conscious mind. Formerly the conscious and developed mind was lacking. In our human evolution, it was the animal mind that was working. Now the animal mind has been transformed into the conscious, developed human mind. Consciously man knows what is right and wrong in his own life. In spite of that, man often does the wrong thing. But now man's conscious, developed and searching mind has become illumined to some extent by an inner light and by his heart's constant cry. [1-26]

Experiencing the Infinite

The One the *rishis* described is not an abstract concept or a deductive theory, but an experience of something that united them with their personal and universal Source. It is the consciousness we term *transcendental*. In Sanskrit, this is *samadhi*, an absolute realm unalloyed with human thought, desire or ignorance. The frame of reference is thus beyond our physical existence and surroundings and beyond the possibility of measurement or susceptibility to the influences of social, economic or cultural bias. It is the drop, the individual consciousness, merging with the consciousness-ocean.

Why should we have faith in this wisdom and in the masters, who experienced and articulated it in the remote past and whose contemporary representatives do so today? Why does Sanskrit, a language like ancient Greek and Latin no longer spoken, need our attention for other than philological and historical reasons? Why should the representatives of secular wisdom: philosophers, historians, scientists and the scientifically inclined give their time and attention to this world view when it appears as just another of the tedious multitudes of philosophies and myths competing for a place in our minds? Where is the proof?

No conventional proof will ever satisfy our minds about what Sri Aurobindo designated as the *supramental* consciousness. To suggest the frame-shift of awareness distinguishing mind and spirit, many masters have used parables to instruct their students. One of the more effective is the ancient story of *The Frog in the Well*. The origins of this tale have variously been attributed to India, China and Greece, but its value remains whatever its genesis. The following version was told by Swami Vivekananda [1-27] in an address to the World Parliament of Religions in Chicago in 1893.

A frog lived in a well. It was born there and brought up there, and yet it was a little, small frog. Over time, it found enough worms and mircoorganisms in the water to eat and grew sleek and fat according to its circumstances.

One day another frog, who lived in the sea fell into the well. "Where are you from?" asked the frog in the well. "I am from the sea." responded the other frog. "The sea! How big is that? Is it as big as my well?" The frog took a leap from one side of the well to the other.

"My friend", said the other frog, "How can you compare this little well to the sea?" The frog took another longer leap from wall to wall and again asked, "Is it this big?"

"You are speaking nonsense, trying to compare a well to the sea" said the visiting frog.

"But," said the frog in the well, "nothing can be bigger than my well; nothing can be bigger than this. You are a liar! Go back to wherever you came from." and he forced the frog to leave.

Once we have experience "outside the box" of a vaster nature, proof in the usual rational modes becomes unnecessary and indeed impossible. The old box is no longer needed because we have a new larger frame of reference. Swami Vivekananda or Sri Aurobindo would tell us that the proof of spiritual Truth is self-evident, based on our experience of entry into that realm transcendent to mind and senses. The frog ascends the walls of his well and beholds the sea.

Realized spiritual masters and their students adhere to standards that are far, far stricter and much simpler than those required of the scientific or intellectual community. They have had transformative spiritual experiences bringing immunity to any pull of the temptation by ignorance. According to Sri Chinmoy and Sri Aurobindo, the culmination of the spiritual quest is a permanent enlightenment, a realization from which one does not descend.

In addition, each successive fully realized master incorporates and expands the realizations of those that have come before. [1-28] All bring messages from the Highest, and all teach the same fundamental inner Truth to whomever has the receptivity to learn. They come only to accelerate and inspire human evolution. Like Krishna, these masters are wont to appear when we are facing the greatest opposition by the forces of ignorance (See note i-7).

To benefit from the yogis' wisdom, we need to have a credible basis for placing value and faith in their experience since they purport to know both divine and terrestrial human life. Should we be drawn into the orbit of any true master, it helps to remember that he or she is indeed human as are we. What they have achieved is something intrinsic to our own nature, something to which we have every right to lay claim and invoke. Through lifetimes of prayer, concentration and meditation, they have gradually surrendered their limited mental understanding to the infinite sea of inner Light, their own expanded self.

As a butterfly emerging from its chrysalis is the transformation and replacement of the caterpillar, so the yogi's unhorizoned consciousness is the transformation and replacement of what had been finite and egoistic. What emerges in the yogi's case is a self-consecrated instrument of the divine Will. Action is still there. Thought and physical needs are still there, but all is directed by the Supreme Will working through the soul within. Uncertainty and insecurity have gone. Doubt has gone, and the analytic decision-making process as such no longer operates. Even expectation is absent.

In this state, masters abide in an eternal present, spontaneous, subject only to the soul-Force within, without personal desires or attachment to the outer world. There is lasting peace, light, and satisfaction, which they experience at every moment. It is from that consciousness that they mix with us, freed from but steeped in fathomless compassion for our normal but narrower human emotional-mental-intellectual perspectives. [1-29]

The fully realized yogis' relationship with humanity, struggling with the forces of ignorance, searching for some degree of satisfaction in life, is expressed through offering hope, love, compassion, and encouragement. They know the pains of life because they have experienced them in full measure on their own journey to enlightenment. They know the landscape of spiritual seeking and are capable of guiding those who are brave, sincere, determined and patient enough to undertake the quest.

The true masters, from whatever tradition they spring, gain a permanent fulfillment in their realization. They seek no outer rewards, praise, wealth, influence, or power. They represent the ultimate *dharma* (a concept discussed in detail in Chapter 5) in its purest form. Their motive, if such it can be called, is simply to offer the world their Light, for they know and see the Presence of the Divine in all of us, even as they have seen and realized that Presence within themselves.

To offer speculation on anything they had not personally experienced or affirmed, they would consider the greatest possible transgression and disservice to their students and to the world. These saintly souls may sometimes seem to be eccentric and are quite often misunderstood and rejected by much of society, but they should never be suspect of their motives.

Sri Aurobindo sheds light on the vantage point of the yogi with respect to his service to humanity and the Earth.

This taking up of the lower parts of life reveals itself as a turning downward of the master eye of the secret evolving spirit or of the universal Being in the individual from the height to which he has reached on all that now lies below him, a gazing down with the double or twin power of the being's consciousness-force, - the power of will, the power of knowledge, - so as to understand from this new, different and wider range of consciousness and perception and nature the lower life and its possibilities to raise it up, it also, to a higher level, to give it higher values, to bring out of it higher potentialities. And this he does not because evidently he does not intend to kill or destroy it, but, delight of existence being his eternal business and a harmony of various strains, not a sweet but monotonous melody the method of his music, he wishes to include the lower notes and, by surcharging them with a deeper and finer significance, get more delight out of them than was possible in the cruder formulation. And that indeed is the true inmost aim and meaning of ethics, discipline and askesis, to lesson and tame, purify and prepare to be fit instruments the vital and physical and lower mental life so that they may be transformed into notes of the higher mental and eventually the supramental harmony, but not mutilate and destroy them. Ascent is the first necessity, but an integration is an accompanying intention of the spirit in Nature. [1-30]

Is it possible for a charlatan or an unscrupulous beginner to pose as an illumined *yogi*? Of course, it is, and they do. The promise is usually a leap of illumination in a short time, provided the student is willing to pay handsomely or otherwise support the teacher (again the profit motive!) A discerning student would be put off by a lack of any of the primary qualities that a real guru should shows: humility, a radiance of purity, peace, spiritual love, simplicity and sincerity. Obligatory payment in the form of money or any material support cannot be and never has been part of the bond between guru and disciple, which is based entirely on inner affinity and mutual acceptance (See note 1-8). Out of love for a real teacher, students may spontaneously and unbidden make love-offerings of money or food or other services within their capacity to provide. Indian scriptures are full of these genuine acts of devotion and gratitude, but it is never a result of a precondition for discipleship or demand by the guru.

It is important to remember that the basis of one's own spirituality arises out of the spark of the Creation-Light within, connecting him to the universal creation. Most of the physical creation is unconscious of this inner wealth. In humanity, conscious aspiration gradually awakens, depending on the number of human incarnations the soul has taken (explored in Chapter 4). At this point, suffice to say that awakening and conscious seeking of inner Truth are slow, evolutionary processes and usually take many lifetimes to mature and bear fruit.

In the Indian tradition, each awakened soul will eventually come under the guidance of a particular master or mentor who is uniquely qualified to guide the seeker to realization. There is an old saying, *"When the student is ready, the master will appear"*, and it is literally true. Consequently, there are people of widely varying spiritual development alive at any given time.

Long before a permanent magisterial illumination occurs, individuals engaged in spiritual practice (prayer, concentration and meditation, selfless service, etc.) have awakenings or intimations of the ultimate goal of their practice. As in Chinmoy's poem (p. 30) one may have momentary flashes of the lifting of all thought and feelings of worry, anxiety, doubt and fear – *A rest immense I enjoy at last* – or of a vastness of mind – *Beyond both knower and known* – or of an aura of love surrounding oneself and the entire world. These experiences of the inner world give us a solid inspiration to continue our disciplines. Accounts from every tradition, irrespective of cultural origin, [1-31] tell us that the depth of these experiences and their frequency increase with practice. Eventually, the glimpses which first announced themselves as fragmentary events, begin to have an integrative effect on our entire life. We find that we begin to develop an intuitive wisdom about the sort of activities and lifestyles in which we engage, pursuing those that elevate our consciousness and avoiding those that cater to our lower propensities, make us unhappy or leave us uninspired.

As our identification with our inner dimensions gains strength and confidence, there comes a more and more insistent prompting of our conscience to make our deeds resonate with the transformative process taking place within us. Eventually, we come to know that our individual progress and is part and parcel of the universal progress,

As our consciousness ascends, a transformation takes place in our life, slowly, steadily and unerringly. Sri Chinmoy repeatedly emphasizes this theme throughout his writings – for example:

Transformation is Divinity's only aim. [1-32]

In emptiness and stillness we hear our Lord's transformation-Voice. [1-33]

God's greatest and highest vision:
the complete transformation of man's nature. [1-34]

Light does not work against darkness.
It works for the transformation of darkness. [1-35]

God asks the seekers to transform and not to reform the world. [1-36]

Is Suffering Necessary?

In the ancient Vedic tradition, those seeking realization left society and retired to the forests or Himalayan caves. They gave away their possessions, left their families and renounced worldly responsibility in order to focus exclusively on spiritual practice. Even kings gave over their rule to their sons to enter this contemplative phase of life. Many joined established ashrams with gurus of high stature. In addition, many seekers underwent years of *tapasya* (spiritual austerities) which could include abstaining from food, enduring long periods of pain and discomfort, vows of silence. They understood that these severe penances and sufferings would provide the purification-fire to purge their consciousness of desires, attachment, and wrong past actions.

The Buddha, more than 2500 years ago, practiced self-mortifying austerities for many months, nearly to the point of death, before it was revealed to him from within that he could not gain self-realization by following this kind of renunciation. In the center of Yangon in Myanmar, there is a temple with graphic gilded sculptures depicting this phase of the Buddha's *sadhana*. The images begin with his physical appearance as young Prince Siddhartha and progress gradually to his becoming an emaciated skeletal wraith. Ultimately, he announced to his followers his intention to abandon his *tapasya*. Breaking his long-standing fast, he accepted food from a young woman passing near the place in the forest where the group was encamped. According to legend, all his disciples left him in disgust, accusing him of giving up the spiritual life, a fallen yogi.

Both Sri Chinmoy and Sri Aurobindo have made very clear to their students that in this stage of the world's evolution, penances and *tapasya* of this austere and debilitating nature are not required, and in fact will be detrimental to spiritual progress. Suffering is not on the path to purification or to illumination. It may occur inevitably resulting from our own attachments and indulgences or unavoidable *karma* (See Chapter 3), but we need never court it. Both these modern masters have promoted physical fitness through athletics to build healthy and strong bodies. [1-37] Rather than neglecting the body they teach their students that in order to meditate well and to serve as transformative instruments of inner Light, a healthy and fit body is not only valuable, but really indispensable.

The field of selfless transformative deeds springs not from our own thoughts of what we should be doing, but from inner inspiration. Mind-originated doings are images we create ourselves. While we may achieve the goals that we set for ourselves, they will not bring any lasting satisfaction. They carry with them some subtle expectation of success, reward, and often a sense of pride, vanity, fame or other dressings of our ego. An aspirant's goal is to invoke from within the high consciousness native to him and then direct that light into the body, vital energies and mind; or, he can allow the ignorant aspects of his being to rise into the Light above. In addition, we need to develop a receptivity to our spiritual heart (the portal to our inner wealth). Without receptivity neither of these two illuminating processes can succeed and give guidance to our deeds from the creation-Light deep inside us.

In 2017 and 2018, I was fortunate to attend conferences on spirituality and sustainability in Assisi, Italy, as the representative of both Florida International University and the Sri Chinmoy International Meditation Centre. There were wide-ranging sharing sessions with spiritual teachers and seekers of many different traditions (mainstream religions, indigenous traditions, spiritual centers). We developed a concordance that whatever progress we made individually and collectively in our *sadhana* (spiritual practice and work) would be radiated to the world at large.

This gathering, to a man and woman, was grounded in the experience that we are all connected directly to a common Source. What we felt was needed was a continuous invocation of that Presence as we moved forward and to inspire as many more individuals as possible to join in that growing body of invocation and transformation. So impressive about this group was that it embraced so many different patterns of world-service: teachers, philosophers, UN and NGO workers, organic farmers, community activists, artists, musicians and networkers among many other vocations.

These conferences gave us strong confidence in the theme of this book, a universal hope that has its basis in the Promise of the Supreme Creator to perfect the creation and which is implanted in the soul of every human being.

Today, in the 21st century we are finding more and more relevance of the unrivalled detailed precision of the yogis' discovery of the inner dimensions of human consciousness. How this detailed wisdom, a true spiritual science, can add to the tools we need in transforming ourselves and the world is the subject of the next chapter.

Notes for Chapter 1

1-1.   *Brhadaradya opanishkaad*, 1.3.28, trans. by Sri Chinmoy, 1996. In *Commentaries on the Vedas, the Upanishads and the Bhagavad Gita*, p. 55. Aum Publ., Jamaica, N.Y.

1-2.   Mind occupies all levels of consciousness. The *physical mind* as described by Sri Aurobindo and Sri Chinmoy is that part of the mind that is always immersed in the immediate outer details of life: petty desires, sense of self-image, finances, family, jobs, etc. The *intellectual mind* is a step higher than the physical mind and is able to form abstract and sophisticated thoughts. Neither of these mental levels has free access to higher Light.

Sri Chinmoy's extensive discussions of the nature and limitations of the seven levels of mental consciousness are summarized in detail in Sumadhur's (2018) [*Sri Chinmoy, Fully Realized Master – His Life and Philosophy*. pp. 138-146. Sumadhur Publications, 600 pp.]

1-3.   The *body* represents the physical elemental aspect of our being that obeys the laws of physics and chemistry, embodying in its untransformed state the *tamasic* principle. Transformed, the body is illumined, the chosen instrument of the Supreme on earth. The *vital* is the dynamic life-energy principle which in Nature obeys the Darwinian laws of survival of the fittest and natural selection. In its untransformed state, the vital being is driven by *rajasic* principles, reproduction, aggression, possessiveness and restlessness. The transformed vital is the pure dynamic force that energizes and serves the *sattvic* yogic life.

1-4.   *Physical* here means the combined body and vital consciousness.

1-5.   Sri Chinmoy. 1971. *Songs of the Soul*. pp. 23-24. Herder and Herder New York.

1-6.   The *Ramayana* is the earliest Indian epic and is contemporary with many of the Vedic *rishis*, some of whom play prominent roles in the story. The tale itself tells of the lives of Ramachandra, Prince of Ayodhya, his wife Sita and brother Lakshmana as they live out a 14-year exile in the forests of north India. Eventually they are drawn into conflict with the powerful demon Ravana, who covets and kidnaps Sita. Rama and Lakshmana, aided by their ally, the warrior Hanuman, do battle with Ravana's forces. Ravana is finally slain and Sita rescued. Rama is considered an *avatar* (an incarnation of Lord Vishnu) by many Indians. Every Hindu child is taught the stories and virtues contained in the *Ramayana*.

The *Mahabharata* is a much later epic, which relates generations of conflict between two royal clans, the Pandavas and the Kauravas. Like Rama and Sita, the Pandavas embody *dharma* (living one's life in harmony with the divine Will). Their mentor is Krishna, also an *avatar* of Lord Vishnu. The Kauravas represent the forces of *adharma* (the egotism of desire, aggression, arrogance, wealth and temporal power). The feud ultimately leads to an enormous battle in which the Kauravas are killed and *dharma* has the victory. The *Bhagavad Gita* (The Song of God) is the eighteenth chapter of the *Mahabharata* and takes the form of a conversation between the great Pandava archer Arjuna and Krishna as the two armies are about to crash together on the field of Kurukshetra.

1-7. *Sadhana* is literally a seeker's spiritual work; it is whichever practices and goals he establishes that lead him toward illumination. If a seeker has a spiritual master (guru), the guru will be the primary guide in determining the nature of the *sadhana*. Otherwise, it comes directly from the soul within.

1-8. Both Sri Aurobindo and Sri Chinmoy have written extensively on this relationship. Sri Chinmoy's *Master and Disciple*. 1985. Agni Press, Jamaica, N.Y. and Sri Aurobindo's *Letters on Yoga*, Vols. 1 (1970) and 2 (1970). Sri Aurobindo Ashram Publications Dept., Pondicherry, India, are indispensable references.

1-9. The full text of the lecture is in, Sri Chinmoy. 1998. *Blessingful Invitations from the University World*. Agni Press, Jamaica, NY.

1-10. Sri Chinmoy. 1998. *My Flute*. p. 3. Aum Publ. Jamaica, N.Y.

1-11. Sri Aurobindo. 1956. *The Secret of the Veda*. p. 10. Sri Aurobindo Ashram Press, Pondicherry, India.

1-12. Ibid. p. 4.

1-13. Ibid. p. 47.

1-14. These expressions I abstracted out of context from several hymns of the *Rig Veda*, Section IX. *The God of the Mystic Wine, Parashara's Hymns to the Lord of the Flame, Surya Savitri: Creator and Increaser* and *The Vedic Fire*. trans. by Sri Aurobindo. 1998. in *The Secret of the Veda*, pp. 285-286, 565-587. Sri Aurobindo Ashram, Pondicherry, India.

1-15. Sri Aurobindo. 2004. *Materialism* [in *Evolution*] pp.20-33. Originally published in the journal *Arya* in 1915 and 1918.

1-16. Ibid.

1-17. Kuhn, T.S. 1970. *The Structure of Scientific Revolutions.* xii + 210 pp. The University of Chicago Press, Chicago IL.

1-18. Pliske, T.E. 2017. *Light, Truth and Nature.* 211 pp. Pacem in Terris Press. Washington D.C.

1-19. This idea is most eloquently and briefly developed and presented in B.W. Swimme and M.E. Tucker. 2011. *Journey of the Universe.* xi + 175 pp. Yale University Press. New Haven.

1-20. Sri Aurobindo. 2004. *Materialism.* In *Evolution,* pp. 20-33, originally published in the monthly review *Arya,* 1915 and 1918. Sri Aurobindo Ashram Press, Pondicherry, India.

1-21. Agni is the Indian god of fire, symbolizing also the inner fire of aspiration to know the Infinite

1-22. Ibid.

1.23. For more on this debate, see Rotblat, Joseph. 1999. *A Hippocratic Oath for scientists.* Science **286**: 1475. and Woodley, Lou. 2012. *Do scientists need an Equivalent of the Hippocratic Oath to ensure ethical conduct?* Landau Nobel Laureate Meetings, 29 June 2012.

1-24. Sri Aurobindo. 1991. *Rebirth and Karma.* p. 71. Lotus Light Publ. Wilmot, WI

1-25. Sri Chinmoy. 1996. *Science and Nature.* pp. 11, 24, 29, 37. Agni Press, Jamaica, NY.

1-26. Sri Chinmoy. 1978. *Earth's Cry Meets Heaven's Smile, Book 3.* pp. 72-74. Aum Press, Santurce, Puerto Rico.

1-27. Vivekananda, Swami. 1953. *Why we Disgree,* address given to the Parliament of Religions, Sept. 15, 1893, in *The Yogas and Other Works.* p. 184. Ramakishna-Vivekananda Center, N.Y.

1-28. Sri Chinmoy. 1999. The summits of God-Life: *Samadhi and Siddhi.* pp. 160-173. Aum Publ., Jamaica, N.Y.

1-29. There are extensive descriptions of this state consciousness found in Sri Aurobindo's *The Life Divine.* 1977. Sri Aurobindo Ashram, Pondicherry, India and *Essays on the Gita.* 1997. Sri Aurobindo Ashram Press, Pondicherry India; and Sri Chinmoy's *Summits of God-Life: Samadhi and Siddhi.* 1999. Aum Publ., Jamaica, NY.

1-30. Sri Aurobindo. 1977. *The Life Divine.* pp. 714-715. Sri Aurobindo Ashram Trust, Pondicherry, India.

1-31. Extensive examples and discussions of these experiences are in Sri Chinmoy's *Meditation: Man-Perfection in God-Satisfaction,* revised ed.

2018. The Golden Shore Verlagsges.mbH, Nurnberg, Germany and in Sri Aurobindo's *Letters on Yoga, Vols. 1-2.* 1970. Sri Aurobindo Ashram Publications Dept. Pondicherry, India.

1-32.　Sri Chinmoy. 2003. *Seventy-Seven Thousand Service-Trees, Part 31, 30469.* Agni Press, Jamaica, NY.

1-33.　Sri Chinmoy. 2002. *Seventy-Seven Thousand Service-Trees, Part 30, 29498.* Agni Press, Jamaica, NY.

1-34.　Sri Chinmoy. 1999. *Seventy-Seven Thousand Service-Trees, Part 15. 14812.* Agni Press, Jamaica, NY.

1-35.　Sri Chinmoy. 2004. *Seventy-Seven Thousand Service-Trees, Part 35, 34493.* Agni Press, Jamaica, NY.

1-36.　Ibid. *34403.*

1.37.　Sri Chinmoy discusses the spiritual value of health, fitness and athletics in detail in *Sport and Meditation.* 2012. 196 pp. The Golden Shore Verlagsges.mbH. Nurnburg, Germany and *The Inner Running and the Outer Running.* 2008. 184 pp. Aum Publications, Jamaica, NY.

2

INNER DIMENSIONS

OF HUMAN CONSCIOUSNESS

I n this chapter, we bring together the basic knowledge and dimensions of consciousness bequeathed to us by the Indian spiritual
tradition. In so doing, we need to remember that their origin comes
from the *collective experiences* of realized masters who were able to
anchor on Earth, probably for the first time, a path to the highest levels of reality, love and joy.

In so doing, they opened a door for the entry of beings, powers,
and Truth of those high domains into the consciousness of our souls,
hearts and lives of which we had been at best only partly conscious
before. They opened a portal of Light, which has been continuously
widened and expanded by all the masters that have come after them.
As such, the teachings of these masters represent a lifeline of promise
from the Creator's transcendent vision and plan to our world of human hopes and struggles.

All aspects of modern scientific study have generated a language
of descriptive detail unrivalled in its scope and complexity. As a biologist, I am in awe of this terminology. There are nearly two million
described living species [2-1] and countless thousands of extinct forms,
each with its separate name. In addition, each of the major groups of
organisms has its lexicon of anatomical terms. Having delved deeply
into the study of vertebrates, plants, and arthropods (mostly insects),
my nomenclatural cup overflows.

In like manner, the community of Vedic yogis coined a unique and highly specific vocabulary to communicate the multitude of inner states and relationships they experienced and shared. This was an empirical discovery, certainly, but even more astounding is that what emerged in ancient Sanskrit was *a language of shared experience.* Rather than experiencing disjunct, subjective, individually formed visions and meditations, they found an inner world that, though presenting itself through diverse experiences, was spiritually unified.

This parallels what biologists and physical scientists have found in the multifaceted outer world of universal Nature, unified in its evolutionary origin and basic laws by which it operates. Going even farther, the *rishis* discovered that the inner spiritual dimensions are directly connected to the physical and psychological worlds we know so well.

Not surprisingly, the Sanskrit hymns and mantras of the Vedas can have multiple, layered meanings where the words refer to outer rituals or forms of Nature but are at the same time symbolic of profound inner truths.

One of these is the Hound of Heaven, Sarama. The literal Vedic imagery tells of Sarama the dog who descends to locate stolen cattle (an ancient symbol of wealth) hidden in a dark cave and leads the owners to recover them. Sri Aurobindo's interpretation [2-2] tells us that Sarama is the symbolic messenger of the Truth-Light descending into the ignorance of each human being to awaken and reveal the wealth of Truth-Light, veiled within each of us. Sarama is the harbinger of the dawn of our illumination.

In the most comprehensive sense, basic yogic experience is that creation/Creator is one being, the One without a second, *brahman or parambrahman.* According to the *Vishnu Purana,* [2-3] the story of origins, there are three major aspects or deities of the One. Brahma, with four faces, radiates the creative process in all directions. Vishnu (Narayan) stabilizes and maintains the creation (also acting as the supreme Creator himself), and Shiva represents change, evolution, progress and the destruction of old forms in connection with the creation of new. They are not separate beings but omnipresent simultaneous forces governing the dynamics of the universe as they unfold its journey. In that story, it is clear that Vishnu and *Param-brahman* (The Absolute Supreme) are interchangeable, and of the three, it is He that is the central Source and personage in the drama.

Both Sri Chinmoy and Sri Aurobindo discuss the mystical *Angirasa*, known also as the seven Vedic *rishis (Saptarishi)* sometimes considered the fathers of the human race, though certainly not in the strict biological or genetic sense. They were the chief residents and guides from higher worlds who established the means by which humankind, with spiritual training, could contact and enter those worlds. The stories and legends of these sages tell us that although they may have taken on physical bodies, they also had powerful inner lives and were "at home" on the higher planes of consciousness. The beings (gods, demons (*asuras, rakshasas*), *gandharvas, apsaras etc.*) and visions they encountered there could also assume human form. The *saptarishis* could converse and communicate with them both in the ancient Sanskrit language when they took physical form and walked on Earth, and in the silent language of meditation in the higher worlds.

In common with other major cosmologies, yogis see the creation at one with its Creator, standing upon a primary duality, *purusha* and *prakriti*. *Prakriti* is the palpable manifestation of the created universe: matter, mind, thought, action, life, death, name, form, space and time. *Prakriti* is the feminine aspect of creation, the Divine Mother, and her generative force is *shakti*. Her various primary aspects are the goddesses of power and transformation (*Kali* and *Durga*), majesty (*Maheshwari* and *Parvati*), beauty-harmony-wealth (*Mahalakshmi*) and knowledge-creativity (*Saraswati*).

Purusha is the unmanifest, the Silence, Witness, the Supreme Father, the Source from which *prakriti* and *shakti* emanate. One way this relationship is represented is by the figure of Lord Shiva, who remains in eternal trance atop Mount Kailash in the Himalayas. His conjunction with the manifest powers of *prakriti* is symbolically depicted by Mother Goddess Kali, queen of life and death, standing rampant like a heraldic lion with her foot upon the seemingly lifeless form of Shiva (Fig.1); but, Shiva is the infinite Source, the Source from which all phenomenal existence arises.

Figure 1. Shiva and Kali
(Clipart Portal)

Should Kali remove her foot from him, the creation, universal Nature, would vanish as would Shiva's form and manifestation. Thus, they are coeval, indissoluble.

Kali is shown in a shocking and terrifying form, with a severed head in her upper left arm and a bowl to catch the blood in her hand below. In her upper right arm, she wields a bloody sword and below holds Shiva's trident. Around her neck she wears a garland of severed heads. Although the image is a violent one, it is important to understand the context of the violence.

It is in the domain of the Mother, the physical creation, *prakriti*, that we have spiritual experiences, struggle and make progress toward illumination. Kali represents the power of aspiration, of the invocation of the Supreme Will to come forth from the soul's domain into our outer life, the progressive movement from the *tamasic* and *rajasic* toward *sattvic* life. The severed heads are ignorance-forces (fear, doubt, lust, jealousy, cruelty, greed, etc.) slain by the *shakti* power of the Mother for the liberation of the seeker's soul. The trident is Shiva's staff of divine authority wielded on Earth by Kali as the agent of transformation of the creation in which old forms are destroyed to make way for forms newer and more illumined.

We will revisit this theme in the following chapter when we discuss the message of the *Bhagavad Gita*.

In India, the Divine Mother has the same measure of respect and devotion as the Father. Sri Chinmoy poignantly portrays this the following poem.

I Sing, I Smile

I sing because You sing.
I Smile because You smile.
Because You play on the flute
I have become Your flute.
You play in the depths of my heart.
You are mine; I am Yours.
This is my sole identification.
In one Form
You are my Mother and Father eternal
And Consciousness-Moon, Consciousness-Sun
All pervading. 2-4

The symbolism of the union of the divine feminine (Earth) and masculine (heaven) in the logo of the Sri Aurobindo Ashram (Fig. 2) is in the two triangles, one facing downwards, the other upwards.

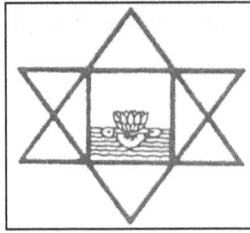

Figure 2. Sri Aurobindo Ashram Logo
(Sri Aurobindo Ashram)

The square delimited by their intersection is Mother Earth (*Prithivi*). Spirit descends into matter (involution) and then ascends through the creation back to its source (evolution). Within the square of the Earth, a lotus floats upon the surface of an ocean of seven levels.

The lotus is the ancient symbol of the human consciousness fully opened to the divinity within. The preferred habitat of real lotuses (*Nelumbo nucifera*) is nutrient-rich pasture ponds, canals and lakes. The root is anchored in the muddy sediment beneath, and the violet and golden flower opens only after it rises to the surface borne on its stem.

The seven levels of ocean represent the seven consciousness-worlds: Gross physical (*bhurloka*), Vital-life (*bhuvahloka*), Mind (*svahloka*), Intuitive mind (*maharloka*), Overmind (*janaloka*), Super-mind (*tapoloka*) and Existence-Consciousness-Bliss (*satyaloka* = *Satchitananda*). The soul must ascend through and claim all seven worlds before it reaches self-realization. The lower three worlds, physical vital and mind (*bhur, bhuvah* and *svah*) make up our normal waking awareness and require purification and illumination before any of the higher levels are fully open to us.

The logo of the Sri Chinmoy Aum Centres (Fig. 3) represents another perspective of the journey toward illumination.

Figure 3. Logo of Sri Chinmoy Aum Centres
(Sri Chinmoy Centre)

The master is standing in a boat in the midst of the ocean, arms outstretched, both piloting the boat and at the same time welcoming new passengers and guiding those already in the boat. In the background is the "Golden Shore" of realization, flooded by the illuminating sun. The ocean can represent the ocean of consciousness as in Sri Aurobindo's logo. As well, the master's boat offers protection from the ignorance-sea that surrounds the seekers prior to arriving at the Golden Shore. The master takes full responsibility for the disciples in his boat, according to their mutual acceptance, and will eventually bring about the disciples' realization in this or in a future life.

Both the cosmic (Sri Aurobindo) and the personal (Sri Chinmoy) elements of the spiritual drama illustrated in the logos are essential to the Indian answer to the question "Who am I?" Full realization reveals awareness of the universal connections innate in human consciousness and the personal role the seeker has to play on Earth as a conscious instrument of the Supreme Will. The teacher or guru is of paramount importance and comes into play when the seeker has progressed to a critical level of awakening. The apotheosis of the personal dimension is in the power of the guru-disciple bond. Once the disciple has realized the Highest, the guru is no longer needed; guru and disciple are one.

Body, Chakras, & Kundalini Power

Our individual soul, *jivatman*, the essence of our divine existence, is the direct representative of the Absolute. In the Game of creation (the divine *lila*) [2-5], each soul has a unique role to play on earth for the manifestation of the Supreme Will, according to its inner potential. It is for this that the body exists. Sri Chinmoy often uses the analogy of a church or temple. Inside the structure is the shrine, the representation of spirit. Without the shrine (soul), the temple (body) is useless and *vice versa*.

Just as a physician needs to know the full anatomical detail of the outer body to properly diagnose and treat disease, a student of higher Truth sooner or later comes to know and experience the inner dimensions of his body. All power flows from within to without, never the reverse. [2-6] The physical body (*sthula sharira*), is connected to the universal consciousness through two inner bodies. These inner bodies are the seat of *kundalini* power, the *shakti* power of the divine Mother. Because the *kundalini* arises in the inner world, it has powers superseding the laws limiting the outer world. Therefore, if revealed in the physical world, we tend to designate these inner powers as occult [2-7] or magical, even though they are normal and native to us.

However, when we manifest them in the outer world, they do not necessarily elevate our own or the Earth consciousness, any more than the activities of eating or drinking would in our waking life. Quite the contrary, if used egoistically or maliciously they will cause great physical and karmic harm to ourselves and to the world. There is a well-known saying, *"power corrupts, and absolute power corrupts absolutely"*, and this certainly applies to misusing our inner powers. We will be breaking the cosmic law and will incur negative and possibly long-lasting karmic consequences.

On the other hand, masters Chinmoy and Aurobindo and others before them have spoken abundantly of the *spiritual power* of the Mother, *prakriti*. Her power is one with *purusha*, illuminating and transformative. The difference between spiritual and occult power lies both in the purity of its source and in the consciousness and intent of the wielder, self-serving or a selfless instrument through which they operate for the seeker's illumination and the world's transformation.

Once we achieve full realization, we receive abundant spiritual and *kundalini* (occult, *siddhi*) powers from the *chakras*. However, realized souls are surrendered instruments, acting obediently according to the Supreme Will for the transformation of humanity and the Earth. Misuse is never an issue for these masters. Sri Chinmoy has commented extensively on these powers as both an inspiration and a caution to spiritual aspirants. Speaking of himself and other realized masters,

> *They use occult power secretly, inwardly, so that nobody can see it. They do not make any outer statement. As a matter of fact, there is not a single spiritual master of the highest order who does not use occult power inwardly. But outwardly if you show occult powers, then you will be in serious trouble. You will not help anybody; you will only feed people's curiosity. And tomorrow if you do not show or cannot show occult powers, then you will lose those followers.[2-8]*

and

> *In my own personal opinion, occultism has to be seen as something very sacred and precious. It has to be reserved for aspiring humanity, because if it enters into the social and political life it will immediately lose its purity and serenity. Then it will not be of any spiritual service to mankind. Spiritual occultism, pure occultism, to which I am referring, has to be used only for aspiring humanity.[2-9]*

> *There is not a single day when spiritual masters do not use occult power in the inner world for the betterment and enlightenment of mankind.[2-10]*

This being said, closest to the physical body is the subtle body, sometimes called the astral body (*sukshma sharira*). The subtle body's primary function is to receive *prana* (life energy)[2-11] from the universal consciousness and distribute it to the physical body. There are three principal channels through which *prana* flows, *ida, pingala* and *sushumna* which are part of the system of the subtle body's nerves (*nadis*). *Ida* rules the left side of the body and the left nostril, and *pingala* rules the right side of the body and the right nostril. *Sushumna* carries *prana* in the central part of the spinal column. *Ida* has an astrological connection with the moon and the planet mercury, and its energy has the qualities of coolness and mildness. *Pingala* is connected to the sun and Mars having energy that is warm and dynamic. *Ida, pingala* and *sushumna* meet together in six different places along the vertical axis of the spine. Each confluence is the location of a *chakra*, a center of inner strength and capacity (Fig. 4).

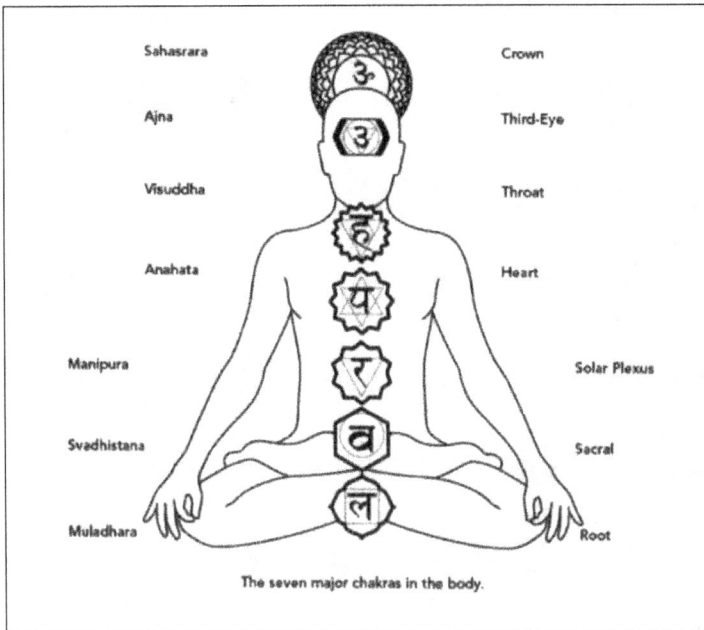

The seven major chakras in the body.

Figure 4: Positions of Chakras in Subtle Body
(*Simple Wikipedia*)

Beginning with the *chakra* at the base of the spine, they are in ascending order:

1. *Muladhara Chakra.* Known as the root *chakra*, *muladhara* is identified with the physical world (*bhur*). If one has mastery over this center, great powers of healing are conferred, but as with all higher powers, they may be safely used only if one has the sanction of the Divine or the soul to do so. One must be able to determine whether the ailment of another person is a necessary karmic experience, which will eventually lead him to a deeper spiritual awareness, in which case it should not be treated.

2. *Svadisthana Chakra.* This chakra is connected to the vital emotional world (*bhuvah*) and bestows the power of love, the power to love others and to be loved by others and by animals. If misused by those seeking a higher consciousness or a life of service, the sexual energies can commandeer the seeker's existence and take him far from the path of illumination. Sri Chinmoy advises that during meditation, one needs consciously to bring light from the heart *chakra* into this center to transform its capacities into selfless, divine love and dynamism.

3. *Manipura Chakra.* This is the well-known navel chakra, the solar plexus, and is connected to the dynamic world (*svah*). Mastery over this center can bestow alleviation of all of life's suffering and sorrow. It can also give the vision of the planes of consciousness to which friends and family have gone after death. The inevitable *caveat* for misuse of these powers also applies here, destructive karmic effects, the creation of inner obstacles and a delay of spiritual progress.

    This center has control over aspects of our personal power and boundaries, the unillumined ego's sense of aggression, territoriality, authority, name and fame. This pranic hub sustains all our tissues from gross to subtle, and it is from here that the energy of digestion and assimilation of nutrients is housed as well as the assimilation and ordering of experiences we have in the outer world. Like the two lower *chakras, manipura* needs purification in order to function positively in the world.

The energies of *svadisthana* and *manipura* govern the activities of the animal kingdom, and they operate powerfully in human consciousness as well. Sri Chinmoy and Sri Aurobindo refer to them as the *vital* aspect of our being.

4. **Anahata Chakra.** The heart lotus takes its name from the presence of the sacred sound of creation, *Aum*, which can be experienced there during deep meditation. *Anahata* means "unstruck," and *Aum* is named by the yogis as the *anahata nada*, the unstruck sound, self-generated needing no external force. For us, the heart is the most important *chakra* for the spiritual transformation of our lives and the direct communication with our own soul. Both Sri Chinmoy [2-12] and Sri Aurobindo [2-13] identify this center as the quickest to gain safely the soul-experiences that are required for spiritual progress. From the heart, inner delight, vastness of the universal consciousness, the essence of Nature's beauty and oneness with whatever or whomever is the object of our concentration are given to us. Both modern masters encouraged their students to use the heart center as their initial point of concentration during their prayer, meditation and service. It is here that humanity's next big leap in awareness is to come and the beginning of our highest realization of what it means in fullness to be human.

This center is safe in every respect save one, and the seeker need have no fear if the radiant qualities of this *chakra* come into his life. The only warning comes from the heart's power of inner "astral travel" where a person can separate soul from body and travel to any part of the universe he wishes. If this is inwardly sanctioned by your master or your soul's will, then no harm will come, but if inner travelling is done out of ignorant curiosity or maliciousness, the contact between soul and body may be irreparably broken, and the traveler can never return home. A word to the wise.

5. **Vishuddha Chakra.** The throat chakra is a mild and creative center. It is partially or fully open in many people. It is from here

that all artistic expression originates poetry: prose, music and art of all varieties. Universal Nature surrenders all her secrets to us, and one can retain youthfulness of mind and body. Messages from the higher planes use this center for expression to the outer world. For those whose service requires this capacity, *Vishuddha* is available and indispensable.

6. *Ajna Chakra.* "The third eye" is located between the eyebrows and a little above. This is a most powerful center. If opened properly one can destroy the ignorant aspect of the past and delete it from the consciousness. Yogis who realize that they may have had unfortunate or unaspiring previous lives use their third eye to obliterate these experiences, since they do not cherish or want to be reminded of them.

This chakra gives the power to see the future and, if it is the cosmic will, to accelerate auspicious events to fruition much earlier than they might otherwise occur. As with all the *kundalini* powers, the misuse of the *ajna chakra's* vision can produce destructive consequences to the user and to others. If we attempt to bring a future condition into the present without taking the blessings of the Highest, our soul or our teacher, our sanity may be affected, and great damage may be done to our spiritual aspirations

7. *Sahasrara Chakra.* The thousand-petalled lotus resides in the center of the brain near the pituitary gland of the outer body. Sri Chinmoy describes his experiences of *satchitananda* (existence-consciousness-bliss) in the crown center as the mystical union of the Infinite, the Eternal and the Immortal, of the Creator and the universal creation, knower and known, lover and beloved, dream and reality, the cosmic Game and the Player Supreme. One comes to know he is birthless and deathless. This *chakra* is the elder member of the family of subtle body centers and troubles not the powers and workings of the lower centers nor seeks to interfere with them. Here the seeker is a surrendered and consecrated instrument of the Highest and has the authority manifest whatever the Creator wants to impart to the creation.

Then, beyond the subtle body and the *chakras* is the causal body (*karana sarira*) in which all the capacities of the subtle and physical bodies exist is seed form, as all the qualities of a tree exist within a seed. This body is at the frontier of the creation/Creator interface, between the universal energy and anything we might call the individual aspect of existence.

Just as the physical body is made up of dense physical elements and the subtle body is made of less dense subtle non-physical elements, so also the causal body is made up of even finer, least dense causal elements.

In exploring our intrinsic inner capacities, it may not be of primary importance to open and experience all the wealth of the *chakras*. Whether these experiences are necessary depends on one's individual spiritual needs or the guidance of a qualified master.

In pursuing *kundalini yoga*, there are two distinct paths, each leading to the opening of the chakras. One is the *tantric* method where the centers are opened one by one, beginning with the lowest and their energies purified to the point where they can be of service to the seeker's progress and to the world. This is a potentially dangerous method and should never be undertaken without the constant guidance of a master. If purification is not accomplished, the seeker may suffer overwhelming aggressive and sexual desires and lose his inner progress, aspiration and mental balance.

The other and safer path is the *vedantic* approach. Here the student undertakes the purification process through prayer, concentration and meditation on the heart *chakra* in advance of entering into the lower centers. Then one can bring the Light of the heart into the lower centers; or the lower vital energies can rise up to higher levels where they can be purified, illumined and channeled properly.

Traditional & Modern Paths of Yoga

Traditionally, there are three major yogic paths that lead to realization.

1. *Bhakti yoga* is the yoga of devotion and selfless love for the Beloved, the guru, the Supreme Lord. Legendary Indian model include the devotion of the great warrior Hanuman for Lord Rama [2-14], the *gopis* and Radha (girl cowherds), [2-15] and later the devotion of Mirabai [2-16] for Krishna. *Bhakti* is common among devotees of many masters and paths the world over. All of the devotee's capacities, physical, vital, mental and spiritual are focused on the beloved in the form of the guru or master or a divine personage such as Christ, Buddha, Krishna or Rama. The goal is for lover and beloved, the finite and the infinite to become one.

2. *Jnana Yoga* is the yoga of discriminating wisdom, which is pursued by attaining higher and higher levels of mind and spiritual expansion in order to arrive at the absolute Truth. This path is exemplified by the writings of Sri Aurobindo and Swami Vivekananda. [2-17]

3. *Karma Yoga* pursues selfless dedicated action and service as the essence of the path. The *karma yogi* aspires to selflessness, self-abnegation and finally self-consecration as a fully surrendered instrument of the Will of the Absolute. The Indian ideal is Arjuna, the great warrior in the epic battle between the Pandava and Kaurava clans on the field of Kurukshetra. Arjuna at first refuses to fight against the enemy, counting among its hosts many of his relatives and former mentors. Krishna is his charioteer and as the embodiment of infinite wisdom, enlightens Arjuna, telling him that it is the Will of the Divine that the Kauravas be destroyed. Arjuna then enters into battle with unshakable confidence and authority. This dialogue is the substance of the *Bhagavad Gita*.

For our times, both Sri Aurobindo and Sri Chinmoy taught an amalgamation of all three approaches suitable in its flexibility for their students, since many are Western and live in the midst of bustling modern urban society. Sri Chinmoy's path (Love, Devotion and Surrender) tends much more toward *Bhakti*, while Sri Aurobindo's (Integral Yoga) leans strongly toward *Jnana*.

For the 21st. Century the role of *karma yoga* is of waxing importance. In the past, many masters and aspirants withdrew from society to seek illumination in the solitude of Nature or a closed *ashram* community. If they were concerned about the transformation of the world consciousness, they made their efforts in the inner planes rather than by direct outer activities. The modern masters, Sri Aurobindo and especially Sri Chinmoy, taught that whatever spiritual progress one had made, it should be *manifested* in all the outer life's actions at every moment. This is true whether a seeker is young or old, raising a family, working in an office, a teacher, construction worker, artist, musician or an activist working for a higher cause. Each has a role to play. Each is indispensable.

Both Sri Chinmoy and Sri Aurobindo frequently answered a question from their students, which in general terms is *"Why is it that when I began my spiritual practice I found that all my negative thoughts, desires and feelings came forth with great intensity to challenge my progress? Am I doing something wrong?"* Both masters have answered this question in much the same way, and while responses to individual seekers address their personal spiritual development, their answers apply both to the level and *sadhana* of the individual posing the question, and to the evolution and transformation of the world consciousness. The following answer [2-18] given by Sri Chinmoy to a guest at one of his public lectures is a comprehensive example. Although the guest's question is about America, the principle applies to all nations in the context of their individual national histories and spiritual development.

When we consciously open ourselves to the Light, inevitably all our unconscious weaknesses and limitations come forward to bar the way. The more the Light beckons us, the stronger become our unruly, undivine and unconscious parts. This is an inescapable spiritual law, which we can see operating in the individual as well as in the collectivity. Before proceeding to your question about America, let me explain why this law exists.

Ignorance has always ruled the Earth, and even now it dominates the Earth-consciousness. The material world has not consciously aspired

for its own inner fulfillment, which is part of an integral spiritual
fulfillment of humanity. Darkness has always been the master. It does
not want a higher force to take its place, so it fights with all its power
to perpetuate its rule. And so, when the divine force succeeds in mak-
ing an opening in a certain area of the Earth-consciousness and is
rewarded by renewed aspiration, the undivine forces also intensify
their efforts, creating values and ideas which are utterly empty of any
higher truth. This eternal battle between darkness and Light becomes
even more intense when a new and higher cycle is about to begin in
the evolution of mankind, which is the case today.

These are the primary reasons for your feeling that a yawning chasm
exists between America's high aspiration and ideals on the one hand,
and some of her unlit actions and values on the other. Her evolving
spiritual awareness and her hasty outer movements are not quite in
collaboration with one another. Until the Light dawns fully, the true
seeking cannot come forward wholeheartedly; hence the values lead-
ing to integral spiritual progress are not much in evidence.

America, moreover, is a young nation. It does not want to walk; it
wants to run as fast as possible in order to breast the tape first. You
know that while running at top speed there is every possibility of
stumbling or running off the track. Nevertheless, with America's sin-
cere and dynamic urge for progress, her present gropings and wan-
derings will pale into insignificance as we vision the promise and
possibilities of her future fulfillment.

This law governing evolutionary progress in an aspect of the process of inner purification, necessary to manifest lawfully the divine
qualities that our inner potential confer. We will come back to it again
in the following chapter, for it is the central concern of the *Bhagavad
Gita*, which, like the Vedas and Upanishads is one of the pillars on
which he Indian spiritual tradition rests.

Notes on Chapter 2

2-1.   Most biodiversity indices currently give the number of described species as about 1.5 million, but estimates for the total number must lie between 7.7 and 10 million. Species living the canopies of tropical rain forests, tropical marine ecosystems and in soils (particularly microorganisms) are still incompletely explored. It is a sobering thought to note that the U.N. recently announced that an estimated 1 million species are currently in danger of extinction.

2-2.   Sri Aurobindo. 1998. The *Secret of the Veda*. pp. 211-222. Si Aurobindo Ashram Press, Pondicherry, India

2-3.   *The Vishnu Purana*. 2015. Trans. by H.H. Wilson and written and published by Rigvedic Maharishi Parashara. The early stages of the creation of the Earth and mankind are written in terms of the inner dynamics of the earliest *angirasas* and the creative visions of Vishnu in forming the spiritual and physical nature of Earth. There is no clear distinction between the inner and outer personages of these masters. What emerges is the incarnation or at least a physical presence of great rishis who could appear, interact with and instruct aspiring human beings to establish the basis for Vedic wisdom, society and ritual.

2-4.   Sri Chinmoy. 1972. *My Flute*. Aum Publ. Jamaica, N.Y. p. 57.

2-5.   *Lila* literally means dance, i.e. the Dance of Life. These are the evolutionary movements of universal Nature and the Earth in its inexorable movement from ignorance to integral realization.

The universal *lila* is sometimes represented by Lord Shiva (as *Nataraja*, Lord of the Dance) dancing within encircling flames. The dance has its destructive as well as its creative aspect, since old forms are continuously being destroyed both inwardly and outwardly as more perfect forms are created and manifested.

2-6.   My descriptions of the body, the chakras and their powers, draw upon three sources, all of which serious students should consult in their study: Sri Chinmoy. *Kundalini, the Mother Power*. 1974. iv + 106 pp. Aum Publ. Jamaica, N.Y.; Sri Chinmoy. *The Body, Humanity's Fortress*. 1974. Agni Press, Jamaica, N.Y.; and Sri Aurobindo. 1977. *The Life Divine*. 1114 pp. Sri Aurobindo Ashram Press, Pondicherry, India.

2-7.   The term *occult* is derived from the Latin *occultus* meaning secret or hidden. In popular culture it has connotations of darkness or sorcery because these powers have often been used to manipulate or intimidate others against the Will of the Supreme Creator. Sumadhur (2018)

in *Sri Chinmoy, Fully Realized Master* p. 60 reports that Sri Chinmoy used the term to refer to various esoteric powers or *siddhis* acquired by opening the *chakras*. At times, he also used the term *Kundalini power* or *psychic power* in the same context.

2-8.   Sri Chinmoy. 2013. *My Golden Children.* p. 8. Agni Press, Jamaica, N.Y.

2-9.   Sri Chinmoy. 1977. *Occultism and Mysticism.* Agni Press, Jamaica, N.Y.

2-10. Sri Chinmoy. 1998. *Seventy-Seven Thousand Service-Trees, Vol. 5*, poem 4090. Agni Press, Jamaica, N.Y. An extensive discussion of Sri Chinmoy's philosophy and experience with inner power can be found in, Sumadhur. 2018. *Sri Chinmoy, Fully Realized Spiritual Master.* pp. 58-72.

2-11. *Prana* is part of the universal cosmic energy, synonymous with *chi* in Chinese traditional medicine. It is life energy, life breath and life force. The soul invokes *prana* to enter our physical body to sustain it for several decades. When the Divine Will dictates, the *prana* is withdrawn, and physical death occurs. If we can be conscious of our breath during mediation, it is possible to become aware of our connection to the cosmic breath, the source of our *prana*. When our individual *prana* is in complete harmony with the universal breath, our life becomes fulfilled and realization is on our horizon.

2-12. Sri Chinmoy. 2018. *Meditation – Man-Perfection in God-Satisfaction.* 302 pp. Aum Publ. Jamaica, N.Y..

2-13. Sri Aurobindo. 1970. *Letters on Yoga, Part II.* Pp. 503-872. Sri Aurobindo Ashram Press, Pondicherry, India.

2-14. Hanuman is the divine warrior-helper of King Ramachandra of the *Ramayana* epic. He is depicted as a monkey, although probably he was a member of one of the indigenous tribes inhabiting southern India at the time. He is a true *bhakta* (devotee) who has identified himself completely with Rama's blessings and power. Having acquired tremendous occult capacities through his oneness, he is instrumental in the defeat of the demon Ravana and rescuing Sita from captivity. He is often depicted opening his heart which contains only the images of Rama and Queen Sita, whom he considers his true father and mother.

2-15. The *Vishnu Purana* and the *Sri Bhagavatam* describe the life of Krishna on Earth. As a youth, Krishna lived in the countryside surrounding Vrindiban as a cowherd. Radha and her companions, the *gopis* (cowherds) were his companions when they took their families' flocks out to graze. Radha's love for Krishna was of surrendered spiritual oneness with her Beloved. The couple is a symbol of the divine purity and perfection of spiritual love, and Radha is one of the paragons of womanhood taught to all Hindu children.

2-16. Mirabai (1498-1557) was a Rajasthani princess who married into a royal family who were devotees of the Divine Mother. Mirabai felt love only for Krishna, whom she considered her true husband. After several unhappy years of marriage to the prince, she left for Vrindiban, Krishna's sacred home. There she spent the remainder of her life, attracting devotees from all over India, meditating and composing and singing *bhajans* to Krishna. According to legend, Krishna appeared to her in subtle form, visible to her but not her companions, and fulfilled her wish by opening his heart chakra and taking her physical body into his being.

2-17. Swami Vivekananda (1863-1902) was a close disciple of the great Bengali master Sri Ramakrishna (1836-1886). He was the first Indian *yogi* to visit America, making presentations at the Parliament of Religions in Chicago in 1893. Over the next decade he traveled extensively through the American east and midwest and in Europe giving talks on Vedanta and establishing spiritual centers. He guided many disciples, some of whom returned to India with him to work for the transformation of Indian society, particularly women's rights.

2-18. Sri Chinmoy. 1971. *Yoga and the Spiritual Life.* pp. 67-69. Aum Publ. Jamaica, NY.

3

ORIGINS AND EVOLUTION

Self-transcendence is the only goal of the tree of life. [3-1]

Sri Chinmoy

Inner Origins

L ike all aspects of the outer world, the origins of humankind, the Earth and the universe lie not in strictly physical processes of astrophysics, chemistry, geology and biology, although there is no quarrel with the reality of the objective scientific account. The deepest origins arise from the inner creative processes of the universal consciousness, eventually manifested in physical terms. This is the basic formula of proceeding from the inner worlds to the outer.

The creation of Mother Earth (*Prithivi*) as described in the *Vishnu Purana,* [3-2] proceeds from the cosmic ocean of consciousness, from which it was raised by Vishnu himself. The narrative takes the form of a series of answers by the sage Parasara to questions posed by his disciple Maitreya. It is told again and again that every aspect, every atom, every nuance of form and intent of the Earth is fully encompassed by the Will of its creator, Vishnu, and by implication that all is bound together by the hallowed bond of divine love and compassion.

71

The *Vishnu Purana* tells us further that Mother Earth takes her foundation from earlier Earth-existences, which were mostly dissolved or unmade in previous *kalpas* (eras). In our present condition, Earth's essence and subtle substances have been assembled according to the vision and dream of Vishnu, which encompasses the movements of every event, being and evolutionary process from beginning to the ultimate apotheosis in which the entire terrestrial creation *consciously* and perfectly embodies the oneness-dream originally envisioned. A passable metaphor would be the planting of a seed destined ultimately to grow into a perfect mature plant.

Besides the elemental substances of the Earth and universe, time is also a property of the creation. Since there is movement along a progressive course toward fulfillment, time comes into being as an inevitable accompaniment. Prior to the creation, in the pure consciousness of Vishnu, time had no existence. *Vishnu Purana* makes very clear that the will of the creator from the very first, is that darkness and Light will coexist on Earth. The Creator is all Light, and beyond the three *gunas*, but chooses to implant darkness into his work with the Earth, with the goal of its illumination. Thus, two principles of evolution are born, progressive illumination and transformation.

Vishnu imbued his universal creation with three successive stages of manifestation, the three *gunas*. These are *tamas*, the principle of darkness, ignorance, inertia, helplessness and avoidance; *rajas*, the principle of action, passion and struggling emotion; and *sattva*, the mode of illumination, peace, knowledge, satisfaction and fulfillment. On whatever plane of consciousness, we focus, *tamas* evolves gradually through *rajas* inexorably toward *sattva*; and in the highest supreme realization, even *sattva* is transcended. Light does not destroy darkness; it transforms it. Sri Aurobindo captures this basic principle succinctly, in his analysis of the meaning of the *Bhagavad Gita* [3-3]

The message of the Gita is the gospel of the Divinity in man who by force of an increasing union unfolds himself out of the veil of his lower Nature, reveals to the human soul his cosmic spirit, reveals his absolute transcendences, reveals himself in man and in all beings.

The potential outcome here of this union, this divine Yoga, man growing towards the Godhead, the Godhead manifest in the human soul and to the inner human vision, is our liberation from the liberated ego and our elevation to the higher nature of a divine humanity.

This is not simply a silently beautiful transformation like the opening of a lotus from a bud. It is in essence a battle between the higher and lower forces latent within us, what Sri Aurobindo describes as,

.... the struggle of which the world is the theatre, in two aspects, the inner struggle and the outer battle. In the inner struggle, the enemies are within, in the individual, and the slaying of desire, ignorance, egoism is the victory. But there is an outer struggle between the powers of the Dharma [3-4] and the Adharma in the human collectivity. The inner is supported by the divine, the godlike nature in man, and by those who represent it or strive to realize it in human life, the latter by the Titanic or demoniac, the Asuric and Rakshasic nature whose head is a violent egoism, and by those who represent and strive to satisfy it. This is the war of the Gods and Titans, the symbol of which the old Indian literature is full, the struggle of the Mahabharata of which Krishna is the central figure being often represented in that image; the Pandavas who fight for the establishment of the kingdom of Dharma, are the sons of the Gods, their powers in human form, their adversaries are incarnations of the Titanic powers, they are Asuras. [3-5]

Sri Chinmoy brings this into the immediacy of today's world and the intimacy of our personal lives.

The battle of Kurukshetra was a real battle. It did take place over 4000 years ago. Krishna was there in human form; Arjuna was there. It is absolutely true, and this battle is taking place every day deep within us between the divine forces and the undivine forces in us. Since we are seekers, ultimately the divine forces within us will gain victory. Also in the case of the Gita the Pandavas did win the battle. If we are not seekers, the undivine forces will go on winning and keeping us

under their control. But since we are seekers, we are bound to con-
quer our undivine, hostile and unaspiring forces. In the battlefield of
life, we are bound to win because we are aspiring. 3-6

In the inner planes, the beings of all levels are created: gods and
goddesses (*devas*), demons (*raksashas*), celestial musicians (*gandhar-*
vas), nymphs (*apsaras*) and countless others. Even the Vedas at first
take an inner form as divine personages who will later descend to be
revealed in physical terms to the *rishis* destined to receive them. In
like fashion, the five senses and all the qualities of human consciousness, both positive and negative (e.g. courage, love, wisdom, purity,
magnanimity; pride, greed, lust, hate, aggression etc.), the forms of
worship and sacrifice, the strata of human society and all the biodiversity of plants and animals and their ecological relationships come
into being 3-7. In short, from the minutest detail the Supreme exists in
every part of the creation. Nothing is left out; nothing is left to chance;
nothing is left to proceed on its own, unguided.

In the *Bhagavad Gita*, Arjuna asks a boon of Krishna to reveal his
universal form. Krishna obliges by opening Arjuna's *ajna chakra*
(third eye) and giving him the vision that he requested. Arjuna has
been familiar with Krishna to this point as a kind and wise friend,
companion, teacher and counsellor. When he sees the full inner
power of Krishna as the *mahapurusha* (Lord of the universe) he draws
back shocked, paralyzed, dumbfounded. He is overwhelmed by
thousands of flaming beings and wheels with innumerable fiery eyes,
swords, mouths with crushing jaws. He sees the creation and destruction of *asuras*, great warriors, kings, kingdoms, and cities in the
arena of universal Nature, vast beyond description or comprehension. In awe and terror, he shrinks back from the dreadful pano-
rama.3-8

What Krishna has shown him is the constant destruction of undivine beings and old forms, old human accomplishments making way
for the simultaneous creation of new forms better representing the
divine evolution of the universe. Creation is always accompanied by

destruction. All this is laid bare to Arjuna. He comes slowly to understand that the kind, mild, peaceful and blissful qualities of the Supreme are but one side of Truth. God is present in all aspects of the universe, and to be a perfect instrument of the cosmic Will, requires acceptance of both aspects. Arjuna belongs to the warrior caste (*kshatriyas*), and it is his duty to fight on the side of *Dharma* in the battle of Kurukshetra. All the beings he is destined to slay in battle are already slain in the inner world by Krishna. Once he overcomes his attachments to his personal image of what his duty is and how it is to be carried out, he surrenders his personal will to Krishna's Supreme Will, and rides into battle in perfect poise and confidence.

Scientific Evolutionary Theory
& its Implications

Fundamental to the yogic view of universal nature is that the entire system, including man, is inexorably evolving under the aegis of the Creator toward both a higher physical and spiritual perfection, the divine *lila,* the play of the Creator. Humanity is part and parcel of the universal process, and although we can claim no separate origin or destination. However, we can and must claim the conscious awareness of our position and at the same time of both our origin and destiny. Most significantly, we must also claim the responsibility for choosing to accelerate our personal and collective progress toward the ultimate Goal. Our task includes inner awakening and awareness and dedicated action, which takes its impetus from that spiritual awareness. Sri Aurobindo leaves no doubt about our connections to Earth-nature,

> *Whatever soul there is in man is not a separate spiritual being which has no connection with the rest of the terrestrial family, but seems to have grown out of it by taking up of it all and exceeding of its sense by a new power and meaning of the spirit. This is the universal nature of the type man on Earth, and it is reasonable to suppose that whatever has been the past history of the individual soul, it must have followed the course of the universal nature and evolution.* [3-9]

Before we take up anything of the inner dimension of evolution which necessarily includes the relationship of the soul to the inner and outer aspects of Nature, we need to begin with the more familiar, but to some still controversial, scientific theory of physical and biological evolution, which is so essential to our minds' seizing upon the integrity of Nature. It is from appreciating the process of evolution in the familiar outer forms of such marvels as humankind, parrots, butterflies and rainforests that our appreciation of Nature's inner workings can be amplified and strengthened.

Whatever our personal disposition toward evolution, in the most general terms, if we do have faith or have had intimations that there might be an inner reality and a higher consciousness at the source of things and directing progress, we must consider once again the wisdom inherent in the aphorism *"As above, so below"* taken from the *Emerald Tablet.* [3-10] If we can observe progressive and expansive change, an aspect of maturation and self-transcendence in ourselves, in society, in the arts, philosophy or in Nature, it should prod us to look deeper and more seriously to consider that an evolutionary quality, a quality of self-transcendence, is a primary capacity, even perhaps *the only capacity* of our existence.

If not, then we must explore the alternative, contrary to our honest experience, that we live in a cosmic stasis, such as the purgatory depicted in James Joyce's novel *Ulysses.* [3-11] There, fixity is the norm, everything proceeding in unchangingly familiar, if sometimes bizarre, patterns and cycles, an endless repetition, whereas Shakespeare tells us in Macbeth. we all *strut and fret our hour upon the stage and then are heard no more.*

Over the past several centuries, Western science has come to the collective position that the best way to understand Nature, whether through physics, geology, chemistry, or biology, is to focus exclusively on her outer forces, forms and movements – to be objective. This singularity of concentration has been justified by the apparent immutable regularity of so many natural phenomena, the fundamental laws by which the universe operates. The laws of gravity, motion, energy, and chemistry were elucidated first, followed by those of life and most recently of time and space. Beside the apparent mechanistic appearance of so many phenomena, there is the vast and nearly incredible integrality with which these laws operate in universal coexistence. The universe seems intelligent, but how and from what does the intelligence arise; from whence does our own intelligence arise?

Nothing begs this question more insistently than the theory of biological evolution. That the theory should have been proposed by two different contemporary English scientists simultaneously, is indeed remarkable and certainly not coincidental, if we accept the yogic view of life. Both Charles Darwin (1809-1882) and Alfred Russell Wallace (1823-1913) had similar experiences [3-12] studying indigenous human culture and ecology and observing and collecting tens of thousands of birds, insects, plants and fossils. Both men were immersed in the presence and detailed workings of Nature for many years, and both had powerful and transformative experiences in the process.

To travel as extensively as these two men did was the mid-19th century the equivalent of going into space in the 21st. They saw the planet from a vastly expanded perspective. Both men realized that the thousands of species they observed all showed variation of form within what they considered the biological boundaries of a single species. In Darwin's case, it led him to believe that contemporary life forms exhibited patterns laid down in the remote past, but which gradually changed over time. This is exactly what he saw revealed in fossilized life. Everything so far discovered bears some relationship to existing species.

In Wallace's case, he realized that the supposed fixity of species' forms varied from place to place, from island to island, and by inference had done so over great spans of time. Initially limited ideas and facts found a theater of expansion in both their minds, revealing patterns of temporal continuity within planetary life, a continuity hitherto undetected or only vaguely suspected.

Darwin, a professed agnostic, refused to speculate on any metaphysical implications of his theory. He consciously chose to defend his ideas from his unshakable faith in established objective scientific methods. His arguments remained firmly rooted in factual, material observations, enormous volumes of which were at the forefront of his mind and in his personal library.

Anyone who has read Darwin's books and papers will discover that he collected every datum possible before drawing any conclusions or formulating a theory. He corresponded voluminously with colleagues all over the world and went to great lengths to be sure of his facts. Where he was not sure, he qualified his statements as needing additional evidence or carried out the needed observations or experiments himself to strengthen his arguments. Because of his thoroughgoing research methods, he was able to support the concept of evolution by natural selection with such scientific rigor and depth that he convinced many initial skeptics. By the time of his death in 1882, a great majority of the most influential natural scientists had accepted the theory.

A brief recapitulation of the Darwin/Wallace synthesis of theory includes the following points, all of which are held true today by virtually all life scientists.

1. The Earth is very, very old

This is necessary to accommodate the evolution of contemporary biodiversity by the extremely slow process of natural selection from life's ancient beginnings. By Darwin's time, geologists were promoting the idea of uniformitarianism, that the slow processes of orogeny (mountain building) erosion, volcanic activity and sedimentation had been going on not for a few thousand years, but for millions upon millions of years, perhaps eternally, in the endless cycles of Earth's changing form. One of Darwin's Cambridge mentors was Charles Lyell, whose *Principles of Geology* Darwin took with him on the *Beagle*. Lyell passed to his pupil an expanded temporal canvas. Darwin himself roughly estimated the age of the Earth to be "several hundred million years" based on his estimations of the time needed to produce the variety of species we observe today. After he published *On the Origin of Species* (1859) [3-13], he was challenged by physicist William Thompson (aka Lord Kelvin) on the grounds that Kelvin's data on gravity and thermodynamics precluded the Earth being more than a few tens of millions of years old. It was a standoff. Neither man backed down, but decades later with the advent of radioisotope dating, Darwin was scientifically vindicated. Today the scientifically accepted age of Earth is about 4.5 billion years. Darwin would probably breathe a sigh of relief. There was scientific proof that there was enough time to get the job done.

2. Individuals within populations of nearly all species show variation of form

Aristotle, the pioneer Greek philosopher-naturalist, had proposed an explanation of universal Nature in which every species had its purpose and existed in terrestrial forms that were immutable. Each species occupied a particular stratum in a hierarchy that became known as the *Scala Naturae*, the ladder of nature. Inanimate forms such as minerals and water provided a foundation for increasingly complex and intelligent forms, including man himself, and proceeding upwards through the levels of deities to the Godhead.

The Aristotelian idea was later combined with the Biblical creation account in *Genesis* to provide one of the major bases for medieval society. Each stratum of society had its place in the hierarchy with kings in closest proximity to divinity (the royal We) and the serf but one step above the animals he tended on his farm. Nature was a divinely ordained ladder spanning deepest darkness to supernal Light and with immutably fixed rungs. Some of the strongest evolutionary theories, including that of Darwin's grandfather Erasmus Darwin (1731-

1802) retained the provision of immutable species within their otherwise contemporary scientific outlook.

Through his own observations and through correspondence with many other naturalists, Darwin became convinced that individuals of all species showed a spectrum of variation of form. There is variety in skeletons, length of limbs, color, size and position of internal, organs, *etc.*, while still clustered within the species' general limits of form and retaining their fitness to reproduce and generate viable offspring.

3. Natural Selection

In Nature, only the fittest individuals survive to reproduce and bear viable offspring, *i.e.* those capable of producing offspring themselves. Here we see the benefit of genetic variation within populations. The larger the population, the more variation; the more variation, the greater likelihood at least some individuals will survive environmental change. Successful or fit individuals have adapted to their environment. Unsuccessful variants do not survive predators, disease, lack of food, competition with other organisms and the vagaries of weather. For Darwin, the vehicles of evolution therefore were populations, not individuals. Populations represented the unbroken continuity of the living evolutionary process, moving forward into the future carrying their proven adaptations and stretching back into the past to the remote origin of planetary life.

4. Environments are in a constant state of change

Darwin's thorough geological training made him acutely aware not only of the necessity of the ancient origin of Earth but also of constant physical changes taking place in all parts of the planet. For example, many of today's terrestrial environments were once under the ocean or supported warmer or colder, wetter or dryer climates as judged by the types of rocks and fossils they contain. All aspects of

Earth's physical existence are in a constant state of flux (the divine *lila*!)

In the early decades of the 20th century a "crackpot" theory was proposed by meteorologist Alfred Wegener stating the Earth's crust was actually a series of plates floating on subterranean magma and behaving like fluids moving in convective circulation. Tectonic plates spread out, collided with other plates and submerged or were thrust upwards, creating zones of volcanic and seismic activity in the process. Over tens and hundreds of millions of years, continents could travel thousands of kilometers carrying flora and fauna along with them. The discovery of sea-floor spreading and fault lines gained wide acceptance of the theory by the 1970s. As with the theory of evolution, there were many doubters because the pace of the movements is so slow. Imagine trying to learn a piece of music with a tempo of one beat every century.

In other words, the rules for survival and adaptation are also continuously changing, no matter where you live, providing a constant stream of new challenges as well as opportunities for all organisms. A successful population cannot rest on its laurels but has somehow to generate new success in an environment of dynamic change. Life is a dance, not an arrangement of statues.

5. All populations are subject to mutation

Since unfit individuals are eliminated from populations and do not pass on their characteristics (genes) to the river of progressive life, there has to be a source of new individual variation that can replenish what has been lost in the relentless winnowing by natural selection. Darwin can have had little or no understanding of the mechanics of such a process, because the laws of inheritance demonstrated by Gregor Mendel (1827-1878) did not become widely known until the early 1900s, two decades after Darwin's death. Still, he knew mutation had to exist. Had he been able to leap forward to the 21st century to grasp the complexity of modern genetics, he certainly would have been pleased to learn in how many subtle and intricate ways the DNA of organisms can influence individual form.

6. New species arise only from pre-existing species

From all the previous aspects of biological evolution, this last and essential part of Darwin's theory was and continues to be the most controversial, especially to those who hold scripturally-based religious views as literally true. Yet, it is also most significant because not only does it state that all species have antecedents which are of similar form and which are their immediate predecessors, but also that species carry with them genetic material that has served their survival for millions upon millions of years.

7. Evolution does not always erase old forms; it may retain or transform them.

Sometimes the characters of new species fulfill the same purpose as in ancestral species, but they may also be modified or combined with new structures to fulfill new functions. For example, human beings have the same basic means of generating cellular energy as most bacteria. That mechanism has been carried along in the currents of evolution for more than a billion years according to current genetic and biochemical evidence. Also, the eukaryotic cell type [3-14] which is the basis of our own bodies is also found in butterflies, amoebae, orchids and catfish. On the other hand, characters that are no longer needed can be suppressed or discarded. It simply depends upon what strategy works best in any given condition.

What was emerging in the minds of 19th century biological scientists in the wake of events leading from the *Origin of Species* was a vision of a flowing river of life that from the present extended back to an unimaginably distant origin and forward into an equally unguessed future. That past forms are carried along variously modified, with the most recent innovations, is the biological principle known as *homology*, well known to Darwin and Wallace. Homologous structures have the primary relationship of common ancestry. This is the glue that holds together the great phylogenetic trees connecting and relating all living and even extinct species. For example, it is possible to trace the human species back through an unbroken lineage of apes and lower primates to humbler mammalian beginnings and thence to reptiles, amphibians, fish, invertebrates, unicellular protists, bacteria, and the dim swirl of large molecules that must have preceded the dawn of cellular life.

The German philosopher and zoologist Ernst Haeckel (1834-1919), had studied homologous patterns of development in vertebrate embryos even before *Origin of Species* was published. When he did obtain a copy and read it, he published voluminous studies supporting the idea of common ancestry. He that coined the phrase *"Ontogeny recapitulates phylogeny."* While it is not strictly true that developmental patterns exactly repeat the evolutionary history of species, since the patterns themselves evolve, there is more than a modicum of accuracy in the poetic aphorism. Haeckel's support of Darwin's theory was instrumental in its wider acceptance.

The irrepressible questions that arise with the ascending chains of form, complexity and consciousness are - what is driving the mechanics of the process, and what is the goal toward which the process of unfolding and moving? Is this simply a process *in vacuo*, the art of a "blind watchmaker" as proposed by Richard Dawkins [3-15], or as Sri Chinmoy and Sri Aurobindo ask us, is there something deeper, more powerful and supremely conscious unveiling itself, opening to the Light? The self-imposed rules by which contemporary science conducts its enquiry cannot answer this question. We need added to it the deeper, higher and wider arena of spiritual experience.

Evolutionary history reveals more a river than a series of plateaus. Form in all species, including our own, moves in the vast, ever-branching, glacially-paced flow of geological time. Thereby, Darwin also introduced the understanding that even in the immediacy of the present, biological form was not fixed. Form was in constant flux, responding to the vagaries of environmental conditions (*i.e.* natural selection) and mutation. Because our perceptions are mostly rooted in the present and our own lifespans, flow and motion through time are nearly undetectable. Again, the river raises the expansion of the metaphoric question. If rivers flow by gravity toward the sea, what power moves the current of evolution and toward what destination?

Even though Darwin chose not to speculate on this, there remains the question of whether he had intimations of a higher power guiding the oceanic vastness of the natural processes he described. Though never explicit, he gave hints. As the theory gained acceptance in the 1860s, later editions of *Origin of Species* contain an increasing frequency, though indeed very sparse, of the words "God" and "creator." In the preface to the sixth edition, he adds an admonition by Francis Bacon:

To conclude, therefore let no man out of a weak conceit of sobriety, or an ill-applied moderation, think or maintain, that a man can search too far or be too well studied in the book of God's word, or in the book of God's works; divinity or philosophy, but rather let men endeavor an endless progress or proficiency in both. [3-16]

In the final paragraph of the book he reflects,

It is interesting to contemplate a tangled bank, clothed with many plants of many kinds, with birds singing on the bushes, with insects flitting about, and with worms crawling through the damp Earth, and to reflect that these elaborately constructed forms, so different from each other, and dependent upon each other in so complex a manner, have all been produced by laws acting around us. These laws, taken in the largest sense, being Growth and Reproduction; inheritance which is almost implied by reproduction; variability from the indirect and direct and direct action of the conditions of life, and from use and disuse: a Ratio of Increase so high as to lead to a Struggle for Life, and a consequence to Natural Selection, entailing Divergence of Character and the Extinction of less-improved forms. Thus, from the war of nature, from famine and death, the most exalted object which we are capable of conceiving, namely the production of the higher animals, directly follows. There is grandeur in this view of life, with its several powers, having been originally breathed by the Creator into a few forms or into one; and that whilst this planet has gone cycling on according to the fixed law of gravity, from so simple a beginning endless forms most beautiful and most wonderful have been, and are being evolved. [3-1]

We may feel that after the decades of one-pointed concentration on and devotion to strict adherence to scientific methods and logic that in the 1870s, when many had been persuaded to accept his conclusions, he relaxed his intellectual discipline and reason a bit and allowed his poetic and visionary capacities to express themselves with more freedom.

We can only wonder what Darwin would have made of the evolutionary theory *cum* Catholic mysticism-based cosmology put forward by the Jesuit theologian Pierre Teilhard de Chardin (See note i- 5) only a few decades after Darwin's passing.

Clearly, if we accept any aspect of spirituality, our satisfactory understanding of evolution in universal Nature demands the acknowledgement of the higher forces acting within the physical theater. Sri Aurobindo envisioned a new birth for science once the inner powers are recognized and given due importance. (ref. pp 36, 42-43)

Inner Evolution:
Death & Reincarnation

The Vedic spiritual vision summarizes the process by telling us that spirit has descended into matter (involution) and will ascend and return to the Light which is its source (evolution). Each soul entering the Earth arena has a prescribed ascending path it will follow through the forms of terrestrial Nature, beginning with the mineral formations and progressing through plant and animal forms before entering into human consciousness and experience.

At first, this looks like a parallel to the emergence of life as described by biological science, but there is a most significant difference. We actually experience inwardly these ascending levels of life through the processes of death and reincarnation.

Sri Chinmoy was once asked by one of his students: "What quality was most characteristic of ordinary human existence." He replied with a single word, *uncertainty*. For we mortals, what is more uncertain than the future, much less death and the hereafter? Who has come back from that unknown realm to tell his tale, or put more truly, whose tale can be believed?

The yogis' experience of the inner worlds is that of evolution, continuity, connection and oneness. Therefore, how could it be that our own existence, part of the universal creation, is confined to several decades on Earth, followed by oblivion? Is illumination and transformation meant for others during a highly fortunate short existence and not for ourselves? In any event, when we enter death's departure gate, there is so much left undone: spiritual aspirations and hopes unrealized, relationships in the process of growth, attachment to near and dear ones, to possessions, projects, world service and desires unfulfilled. In a universe where everything seems to be evolving, an integral flux moving toward a destination and apotheosis, it seems inconsistent and frankly unfair that we should have only a single shot at success and then a finale consisting only of a torn fabric trailing multitudes of severed threads.

The situation fairly demands some path of continuity. Ecological and evolutionary science show us that in physical Nature, there is a definite physical continuity, although it may not mitigate our angst about death and dying. Caterpillars defoliate a plant; lizards eat many of the caterpillars; blacksnakes eat the lizards. Have these creatures disappeared from the ecosystem? No, the plant will spring anew from seeds or new shoots; the moth species will mate and lay more eggs on its hostplants; the lizard species will mate and replenish its population; and even the blacksnake, which itself might fall prey to a hawk, will reproduce itself through other individuals.

When we pass on, our families and relatives continue the lineage of our human presence, even though we do not directly experience the process.

Does extinction occur? Certainly, but again, the lineage of the extinct species is surviving in other evolutionary branches which will undergo the process of geographic speciation and give rise to future species. All the lineages of dinosaurs are likely extinct, but their descendent relatives, thousands of species of birds, delight us on every continent. Nature is radiating renewal and continuity everywhere we look. Physical evolution continues its measured pace through the pageant of all its forms, all transcending and transforming their present shapes and capacities, toward a distant perfection.

Only someone who has the capacity to pierce the veil of this ubiquitous, unknown and possibly inconceivable mystery of inner Nature can be our pathfinder, can reveal how we can and must know death's as well as life's immortality in the secrets of our inmost nature. But what of our individuality? Is it utterly erased by death?

The wisdom of the yogic seers on the subject of death is unanimous. Individual death stopping the flow of personal and collective organic evolution is only an appearance. Continuity is there in the process of reincarnation. Not invented to fill a fearful conceptual gap in an abstract theory, or as a sop to our insecurity, but another of the shared truths Vedic wisdom offers us, one based, as always, upon experience.

Although reincarnation is not yet a fixture of Western science, it is alive and thriving in popular culture. Perusing the "mysticism" section of any large American or European bookstore will reveals dozens of titles dealing with experiences of reincarnation. Some are written be well-known authors and many others are by more humble citizens relating their near-death and afterlife experiences. Science asks, "Where is the proof?" Science has nothing to say on the subject. Yet, reincarnation is a major foundation of Indian and much of Asian spiritual life.

We return again to the *Bhagavad Gita* and the dialogue between Master Krishna and the faltering Arjuna, who is unwilling to go into battle where he will have to kill his cousins, grandfather and uncles. Avatar Krishna is his charioteer and his guru. The metaphor is immediately apparent. Krishna answers all his questions and allays all his doubts. In the process, Arjuna learns the nature of birth, life and death, as Krishna tells him,

> *O Arjuna, certain is death for the born, and certain is birth for the dead. Therefore, what is inevitable ought not to be a cause for thy sorrow.* [3-18]

> *Even as a man discards old clothes for new ones, so the dweller in the body, the soul, leaving aside the worn-out bodies, enters into new bodies. The soul migrates from body to body. Weapons cannot cleave it, nor fire consume it, nor water drench it nor wind dry it.* [3-19]

Speaking of his own journey, Sri Chinmoy reassured all of us: "*My physical death is not the end of my life – I am an eternal journey.*" [3-20] In fact, he told his students that to throw oneself into grief and lamentation on the death of a spiritual master is an insult both to their own and their master's soul, a denial of the soul's immortal status.

In the simplest poetic terms, he captures the quintessential link between the unending process of our individuality and the universal process in Nature. He is not describing the Darwinian machinery of evolution of nature in which humankind is a continuing player but something even more fundamental to both our individually personal and collective inner identity. For Sri Chinmoy, a yogi of modern times, to make such a claim means that he has experienced the truth of his statement – first that death is not the end of the journey, but a transition between episodes of life and, second, that we have not just one but many episodes of life on Earth. Each of us reincarnates, although we may be unconscious of our previous lives or discount the clues life provides.

At first encounter, our minds will tell us the concepts are suspect, speculative, folkloric, unscientific and one more instance of how Eastern and Western cultures differ, and the lack of any scientific evidence or approbation for reincarnation keeps the topic from entering into serious official academic discourse. However, we should remember that the yogic ethics of truth-telling surpass even the scientific peer-review process. So, in the case of Sri Chinmoy, if we trust the storyteller's ethics, then we also have to trust his story.

Of course, there are also further questions of who or what survives death to come again into the world, and for what purpose. In *Death and Reincarnation*, Sri Chinmoy makes clear the Vedic perspective.

Death is not the end. Death can never be the end. Death is the road. Life is the traveler. The soul is the guide. Again and again we shall have to come back into the world. We have to work for God here on Earth. There is no escape. We have to realize the highest here on Earth. We have to fulfill the highest on Earth. God will not allow us to waste or squander the potentialities and possibilities of the soul. Impossible.

Kipling's immortal utterance runs:

"They will come back, come back again

> *as long as the red Earth rolls.*
> *He never wasted a leaf or a tree.*
> *Do you think he would squander souls?"*

Each incarnation is leading us toward a higher life, a better life. We are in the process of evolution. Each incarnation is a rung in the ladder of evolution. Man is progressing consciously and unconsciously. But if he makes progress in each incarnation consciously, then he is expediting his spiritual evolution. Realization will take place much sooner for him than for those who are making progress unconsciously.

We know that we started our journey from the mineral life and then entered into the plant life. From there we entered into the animal kingdom. From there we have come into the human world. But this is not the end. We have to grow into divine beings. Unless and until we have become divinized and transformed, God will not be satisfied with us. So when we think of our evolution – inner evolution and outer evolution – we should get abundant joy. We lose nothing, nothing in so-called death. [3-2]

The spiritual dynamics of what we call birth and death are a symmetrical process. When death occurs, the physical human body returns to the stuff of the Earth by decomposition and recycling the materials from which it was originally fashioned. Students of biology and environmental science will be very familiar with this subject in terms of the action of decomposer organisms reducing the body to small molecules which reenter the biogeochemical cycles that govern the flow of materials in the physical world.

When the soul enters the vital plane, the elements of the vital consciousness and the subtle body are also dispersed into the reservoir of energies and subtle substances that make up that world. Then the soul proceeds through the mental plane where a similar process of divestment takes place, and the elements of the mind and causal body fall away to merge with the cosmic mental consciousness. The same is true for the echelon of the heart, the psychic consciousness.

Eventually, the soul returns to its own world where it is one with the universal Infinite, free from any of the elements of its recent Earth life. Here it resides for a number of years, depending on the progress the soul has made in previous incarnations. However, whatever progress toward illumination the soul has achieved it its past incarnation is preserved permanently and becomes part of the foundation for continued evolutionary progress (homology! See p. 93) in the incarnation to come. Becoming aware of exact nature of the obstructions to progress encountered or obstructed by the body, vital and mind in the previous life, the soul receives a new "assignment" and makes a new commitment to its Source to receive and manifest more Light in its coming life.

Then the soul descends back into the Earth consciousness reversing its pathway taken after death. Passing through the psychic, mental and vital worlds the soul accepts new formations and capacities necessary to carry out its new promise and mission. Finally, having selected a family and environment which have the potential to expedite its progress, it takes on a new physical human form with a new human personality and begins another existence on Earth.

Because reincarnation embodies progressive evolution, once we cross from the animal realm into the human, almost never do we return. It is a one-way trip, according to the yogic view, contrary to some New Age popularizers. Human lineages do not regress into the animal forms that preceded them. Also, in the extensive writings of both Sri Chinmoy and Sri Aurobindo it is clear that whether the soul takes a female or a male body it will continue its journey with that sex, with exceedingly rare exception, in all its future incarnations until permanent realization is attained.

The consciousness of the physical Earth material is *tamasic* and related to the *muladhara* (root) *chakra*, but when it acquires a vital, *pranic* component in plant and animal forms it adds the *rajasic* qualities of the vital, the *svadisthana* and *manipura* chakras. In its impure, untransformed state, the vital engenders egoism in all its forms: aggression, endless desires for power and possessions, passion, restlessness, sexual craving, arrogance, possessiveness, qualities that have survival value in wild nature but are obstructions to entering a higher consciousness.

When the soul emerges from its mineral, plant and animal incarnations as a newcomer to the human world, it carries a strong connection to those experiences and forms. The novice human being comes with all the higher capacities of his species, the outer physical formation, self-awareness and a mind that can develop essential reason and gradual expansion. However, the consciousness is at first

91

largely animal. The vital energies engage the body and mind with aggressive and possessive desires and emotions focused on the prowess and well-being of the individual himself.

Nonetheless, in humankind, *mind* comes forward as the dominant quality of life. While only in a seed form in most animals, mind now functions as a tool to protect, discipline and guide the physical and vital consciousness and also as the gateway to the realm of spirituality beyond the physical. Mind can be instrumental to any level of consciousness. As the *physical mind*, it can be concentrated entirely on the outer life, the urgings of the vital and physical needs and the superficial circumstances of daily life. Here its primary qualities are confusion, insecurity, a feeling of separateness, doubt, suspicion, worry and anxiety. However, with the experiences of more and more human incarnations, the mind begins its evolution and transformation into clearer intellectual pursuits. From there, it moves to an intuitive spiritual awareness of peace, expansion and vastness where the qualities of simplicity, sincerity and purity predominate. Concerns limited to self and family expand to include nation, all humanity, all life, the Earth, the universe. Interest in one's source, thoughts of higher existence beyond the mind, purpose in life, service, happiness and self-giving are all harbingers of *sattvic* mind and life.

When the mind has evolved to a certain extent, it becomes receptive enough to reveal the presence of the *anahata* (heart) *chakra* within. Sri Chinmoy remarks,

> *Now you are crying for joy, but a day will come when your heart is opened, and you will get spontaneous joy from everything. You will look at a flower and get joy, you will look at a child and get joy, you will look at the world and get joy. You will also get peace and the feeling of universal oneness.* 3-22

Once the gateway of the heart begins to open, the soul-consciousness can gradually come forward to descend into the lower chakras to begin the illumination of the body, vital and mind. The soul, the *jivatman,* [3-23] opens the way to the Absolute, the universal consciousness. A soul experiencing this level of awakening will find opportunities to receive guidance through personal prayer and meditation and possibly also through a spiritual teacher. Once the influence of the soul becomes strong enough to guide the "younger members of the family", body, vital, mind and heart, the mind can rise toward what Sri Aurobindo calls the *supramental* awareness, beyond the three *gunas* and into the Infinite.

We are discussing the transformation of the raw, initial human consciousness into a *sattvic,* yogic, illumined state fit to become a surrendered instrument of the Supreme Will. We have been speaking as if it could take only a few months or years, but such a progression usually matures gradually over many incarnations. The guidance of a realized guru will greatly expedite the evolutionary process. Still, in this sense, spiritual evolution of awakened individuals goes at a much faster pace than biological evolution.

Although the caste system of modern India has become an instrument of discrimination, oppression and economic inequality, in Vedic India, the caste system provided a way to organize society so that the degree of a person's inner evolution fit the tasks he would perform. In considering the merits of this arrangement, it is important to remember that in the *Vishnu Purana* this system is one of the *creations* accompanying humanity's appearance on Earth. Also, in ancient society another of the *creations* included the supervision and advisement of rulers, usually endowed with a combination of both *rajasic* and *sattvic* qualities, by established yogis to maintain the *Dharma* of their actions and public policies.

Accordingly, the priestly class, *brahmins,* was proficient in the study of the Vedas and able to give spiritual guidance to lead the religious life and rituals of the community. *Kshatriyas* were the soldiers and often rulers and administrators of their kingdoms, exemplary in their valor, nobility and discipline of vital energies. *Vaisyas* were the merchant and agricultural class responsible for procuring, selling and disseminating goods and services. The fourth caste was the *Sudras* by whose indispensable labor the community carried on its quotidian existence.

Ideally, in its original formation, the caste system mirrored the harmony of the universe in the smooth function of the body of society. Just as each anatomical domain of our individual body, *e.g.* nervous, circulatory, musculo-skeletal and immune systems function in harmony with all the others, all were integrally provided with the basic necessities of life and respected for their role.

If we accept or experience the truth of our reincarnating soul, we must necessarily feel an identification with all stages of the spiritual journey. If we are a novice human being, there is the certainty of hope and the assured promise of growth and fulfillment to come; and, by the same token, if we are more advanced in our wisdom we can empathize with those behind us, knowing we have trodden that path ourselves.

We have deep within us, consciously or unconsciously, a compassion and identification with every human being, every creature, every aspect of the planetary landscape. As participants in the cosmic drama of reincarnation, *we have personally experienced all the forms* and are eternally linked to them through that creation-experience.

We can claim the world, including all its imperfections as our own with an eye to its transformation. Once we see the Creator's Light in the non-human aspect of the world, the creation becomes not just a material environment, but something living, meaningful and fruitful for our own journey. Trees, forests, mountains, rivers, animals all are part of our *experience* in Mother Earth. We have inhabited their forms in past lives, and at a deep level we understand them and love them. Their qualities, needs, and sacred trajectory in the progress of earth-existence are at one with our own. This awakening is a key to transforming our relationship with earth from one of alienation, misuse, and destruction to one of love harmony and beauty.

The Problem of Free Will

As the mind begins to confront the vastness of the spiritual realms beyond its domain, there can arise a temporary disconcerting specter, an apparent loss of individual freedom, of free will. The superficial impression we receive from spiritual evolution is that our personality and individuality will be utterly lost in the overwhelming cosmic milieu of form and movement.

We are the instruments of a higher Force and Will, which is steadily impelling us toward an impersonal distant and unknown goal of cosmic unity. We may feel that this Will is foreign, intrusive, even inimical, an outside presence that is drawing us into a vast mechanism, cold and uncaring. Even though our ordinary lives may be subject to worry, anxiety, fear, frustration, and doubt, we feel that at least our personal situation is familiar and perhaps we have some control over how we proceed.

If we are rational thinkers, scientists, or at least persuaded of the wisdom of science and the primacy of a materialistic world view, then we may want to withdraw and cling fearfully to that view, depending on the facts we already know about the world. This we do even though we are aware that the empirical nature of scientific wisdom is to expand and for theories of the material world to undergo continuous revision to include new discoveries. To a mind used to reason and control of its thought processes, the Infinite can be a scary place, the ocean of the great unknown, and perhaps even the edge of madness.

Plato's *Allegory of the Cave* [3-24] and Swami Vivekananda's story of *The Little Frog in the Well* (p. XX) both illustrate this principle. Once we leave our cloisters of limited perception, we may be at first shocked, but ultimately experience joy in our expanded milieu, not the press of further confinement. Once we taste a wider domain, our smaller world will never again give us the same satisfaction.

We will need to return to this issue, particularly to the icon of free will, in the next chapter, when we will discuss free will in light of the

Law of Karma and its place in our spiritual evolution. Only in relation to that universal Law does free will have value, meaning and fulfillment.

We need the Vedic tradition, the direct experience of the soul through spiritual practice, that can unmistakably give us the assurance that reincarnation is not a deduction, derivative, a calculation or a logical inference from that experience, but an experience itself of self-standing depth and power. All the yogis who have attained the height where they experienced the Nature of the soul's journey understood their terrestrial existence and universal Nature in terms of their own discovery.

Sri Aurobindo stands on that summit and speaks for the millennia of Vedic Truth when he says:

Rebirth is for the modern mind no more than a speculation and a theory; it has never been proved by the methods of modern science or of the new critical mind formed by a scientific culture. Neither has it been disproved; for modern science knows nothing about a before-life or an after-life for the human soul, knows nothing indeed about a soul at all, nor can it know; its province stops with the flesh and brain and nerve, the embryo and its formation and development...Beyond observable fact we must be content with reasonable logical satisfaction, dominating probability and moral certitude, ---at least until we have the sense to observe that there are faculties in us higher than the sense-dependent reason and awaiting development by which we can arrive at greater certainties. [3-25]

The soul needs no proof of its rebirth any more than it needs proof of its immortality. For there comes a time when it is consciously immortal, aware of itself in its eternal and immutable essence. Once that realization is accomplished, all intellectual questionings for and against the immortality of the soul fall away like a vain clamour of ignorance around the self-evident and ever-present truth. That is the true dynamic belief in immortality when it comes to us not as an intellectual dogma but a fact as evident as the fact of our breathing

96

and as little in need of proof or argument. So also there comes a time
when the soul becomes aware of itself in its eternal and mutable
movement; it is then aware of the ages behind that constitute the pre-
sent organization of the movement, sees how this was prepared in an
uninterrupted past, remembers something of the bygone soul-states,
environments, particular forms of activity which built up its present
constituents and knows to what it is moving by development in an
uninterrupted future. 3-26

If we can accept this expansive premise, it opens up and makes sense of many of our experiences that we consciously or unconsciously write off as coincidence or a momentary peculiarity that does not quite harmonize with our ordinary understanding. For example, we sometimes meet people for the first time and have the unmistakable feeling that we already know them, and we wonder how children show precocious abilities in certain artistic activities.

A most notable case is Mozart who could play the clavier with astonishing skill at age two. He performed as a child prodigy in many of the courts of Europe and was considered a phenomenon, a *wunderkind* of his time. How much more sense this phenomenon would make if we knew Mozart was manifesting a mastery acquired in previous lives.

Life on Other Worlds?

In the *Vishnu Purana, Vedas, Upanishads* and the *Bhagavad Gita* and other sacred scriptures of India, all focus is on Earth and the evolutionary process it embodies. There is no mention of physical life on other solar-system planets, other stars or galaxies, although there is repeated acknowledgement of incorporeal beings residing in other planes invisible to us. In an age of science fiction and space exploration, Sri Chinmoy 3-27 fielded dozens of questions about extraterrestrial existences. He has answered all these inquiries in much the same way. I have chosen and combined the following responses because they cover most clearly the greatest scope of our curiosity about this fascinating topic.

The Supreme wants the whole divine manifestation to take place here on Earth, not in Heaven or anywhere else. [3-28] On other planets there is no other plant life or human life. When it is a matter of physical existence, you have to know that it comes only from the five elements [3-29], and these are found only on Earth. But there are living things in other worlds. The soul itself is a living thing. The subtle physical is living, the subtle vital is living, the subtle mind is living. Anything that is in its subtle form is real and has life.[3-30] So, life is in all the galaxies. But life that takes physical form is found only on Earth.

This planet Earth is the world of evolution. Whether we are realized or not, it is here that we evolve; it is here that we make progress. [3-31] Realization is the culmination of the soul's evolution and it can only be had here on Earth. The planet Earth represents and embodies spiritual evolution.

The Buddha, the Christ and all the spiritual masters realized God here on Earth. It is in the physical that we have to achieve and embody the highest states of consciousness….It is absurd to think that someone will attain the highest realization or get illumination after he has left the body if he has not achieved it during his life on Earth. God has to be seen, felt and realized here on Earth. [3-32]

Mother Earth is indeed a sacred world.

Elsewhere, he has said that the cosmic gods, angels, fairies, and other beings native to the inner worlds are fixed in place, performing certain functions in the *lila* but not subject to mortal life and karma or capable of spiritual progress. To enter fully into the drama of physical beings, they would have to take human incarnation and relinquish their immortality. Some beings that have significant power can create for themselves various forms, including human form, speak and interact with us undetected, except by someone whose *ajna chakra* is open.

There is yet another piece in the puzzle of Indian spirituality that we need to explore before we can have the assurance of a complete account of death, reincarnation and the ineluctable evolution toward the highest states of inner illumination. This is the Law of Karma, discussed in the following chapter.

Notes for Chapter 3

3-1.   Sri Chinmoy. 1997. *The Tree of Life.* p. 5. Jharna-Kala Card Co. Jamaica, N.Y.

3-2.   *The Vishnu Purana.* 2015. trans. By H.H. Wilson, written by Rigvedic Maharishi Parashara. pp. 12-39.

3-3.   Sri Aurobindo. 1997. *Essays on the Gita.* Chapters 23-24, back cover. Sri Aurobindo Ashram, Pondicherry, India.

3-4.   *Dharma* is the inwardly dictated course of action and ethics prescribed to the outer life as determined by the soul's inner receptivity to the Divine Will in the context of one's relative spiritual development. This is discussed more completely in Chapter 5.

3-5.   Sri Aurobindo, 1997. *Essays on the Gita.* pp. 174-175. Sri Aurobindo Ashram, Pondicherry, India.

3-6.   Sri Chinmoy. 2015. *Victory to my Supreme.* p. 104. Perfection-Glory Press, Augsburg, Germany.

3-7.   *Devas* are Indian gods and goddesses, usually of exalted status.

3-8.   When Krishna reveals his universal form to Arjuna as Sri Aurobindo describes it in *Essays on the Gita* (Chapter 10, second series, pp. 377-387, see refs. and notes above), it comes as a terrific shock at every level of being. However, this is the real foundation of Arjuna's progress toward non-attachment, an integral knowledge of the world and the true nature of his duty as a *Kshatriya*.

3-9.   Sri Aurobindo. 1991. *Rebirth and Karma.* p. 50. Lotus Light Publ., Wilmot, WI.

3-10.   The *Emerald Tablet* is well-known scripture used by the mystery schools of the renaissance. Its origin is obscure, possibly Hellenic, having appeared sometime between the sixth and eighth centuries in

Arab literature, but likely of much older provenance from China or India. Isaac Newton was fascinated by its mysticism and translated it into English (*MS 28* of Kings College Library, Cambridge Univ. Cambridge, UK.). This translation is available in Pliske, T.E. 2017. *Light, Truth and Nature.* pp. 16-17. Pacem in Terris Press, Washington, D.C.

3-11. According to the analysis of Joseph Campbell (*Mythic Worlds, Modern Words.* 2003. xii + 344 pp. New World Library, Novato, CA.) James Joyce's trilogy of *Portrait of the Artist as a Young Man, Ulysses* and *Finnegan's Wake* is a panoramic and symbolic representation of the spiritual evolution of man based on Homeric, Dantean and Jungian images.

3-12. Darwin's five years on the *H.M.S. Beagle* (1831-1836) as ship naturalist and Wallace's many years spent in the Amazon Basin and what is now Malaysia, Indonesia and Papua New Guinea.

3-13. I am using the sixth and last edition of *On the Origin of Species.* Darwin wrote a series of revisions of the original 1859 edition in response to many questions and clarifications he felt necessary as responses to queries from colleagues in Europe and America and to his own continuing reconsiderations of his scientific theories.

3-14. Eukaryotic cells are generally diploid (containing pairs of chromosomes, one from each parent), have a discrete nucleus and numerous cell organelles in comparison to simpler types of cells.

3-15. Dawkins, Richard. 1986. *The Blind Watchmaker.* W.W.Norton & Co., N.Y. This point of view seems inescapable if one accepts the basic principles of Darwinian evolution and also the rationality of objectivism that currently describes scientific understanding of universal Nature.

3-16. Francis Bacon (1561-1626) was an English philosopher especially linked with the development of the scientific method. Darwin's quotation comes from *Of the Proficience and Advancement of Learning* (1605), acknowledged as a pioneering essay in support of empirical philosophy, which characterizes all of Darwin's own work.

3-17. Darwin, Charles. 1859. *The Origin of Species, 6th ed.* pp. 462-463.

3-18. Sri Chinmoy. 1974. *Death and Reincarnation.* p. 47. Aum Publ., Jamaica, N.Y.

3-19. Sri Chinmoy. 1996. *Commentaries on the Vedas, the Upanishads and the Bhagavad Gita.* pp. 150-151. Aum Publ., Jamaica, N.Y.

3-20. Sri Chinmoy. 2007. *My Christmas-New Year-Vacation-Aspiration-Prayers, Vol 52.* p. 91. Agni Press, Jamaica, N.Y.

3-21. Sri Chinmoy. 1974. *Death and Reincarnation*. pp. 46-50. Aum Publ., Jamaica, N.Y.

3-22. Sri Chinmoy. 2010. *The Jewels of Happiness*. p. 39. Watkins Publ., London

3-23. The *jivatman* is the individual reincarnating soul as compared to *paramatman*, the universal soul.

3-24. The parable of *The Cave* is another famous metaphor for the frameshift in consciousness between ordinary rational mentality and that of inner illumination. See *The Republic of Plato*. 1991. Alan Bloom trans. pp. 193-220. Basic Books.

3-25. Sri Aurobindo. 1991. *Rebirth and Karma*. pp. 5-6. Lotus-Light Publ., Wilmot, WI

3-26. Ibid. p. 11

3-27. As far as I am aware, Sri Aurobindo was never asked such questions. An earlier generation of seekers mostly from the Indian region, with little or no technological or science-fiction cultural focus probably accounts for lack of interest and speculation on their part.

3-28. Sri Chinmoy. 1974. *Samadhi and Siddhi: The Summits of God-Life*. pp. 34-36. Agni Press, Jamaica, N.Y.

3-29. Air, fire, Earth, water and ether. These are the five elements recognized in classical Vedic Indian (and Greek) science (Ayurveda).

3-30. Sri Chinmoy. 1977. *Conversations with the Master*. pp. 38-39. Agni Press, Jamaica, N.Y.

3-31. Sri Chinmoy. 1976. *Sri Chinmoy Speaks, Part 5*. pp. 44-45. Agni Press, Jamaica, N.Y.

3-32. Sri Chinmoy. *A Seeker's Heart-Songs*. 1994. pp. 23-34. Agni Press, Jamaica, N.Y.

4

KARMA & EVOLUTION

The Law of Karma

I f *purusha* is the ineffable soul in its journey of involution and evolution, then *prakriti* with her world of thoughts, vistas, names (*nama*) and forms (*rupa*) is the road travelled. The events of the journey are *karma*. In Sanskrit, *karma* simply means action, but includes thought as well, since thought is linked to action, and both are the domain of *prakriti* and Mother Earth, *prithivi*.

In the common Western understanding, we usually summarize *karma* in the aphorism, *"What goes around comes around"* and *"As you sow, so you reap."* We have a sense of consequence to our actions, despite any formal legal proscription, whether good or bad; and there is a strong flavor of justice, morality, ethicality and even of fate. If your deeds are not in harmony with prevailing ethical norms, if for example you use deceit or violence against others to realize your desires, then that disharmony will revisit you at some point. Conversely, if you have the courage and firmness to obey your conscience, which is hopefully a higher guide for your actions, then harmony will follow upon harmony.

These forces operate in the immediacy of our everyday lives or at least in our current life span or in a number of generations moving together with shared experiences; and in that small limited condition there is some truth to it. Yet, not always.

Sometimes the thief appears never to be caught or punished, the tyrant dies in the midst of his tyranny, without being thrown down, or a pervasive social injustice persists for centuries with no end in sight. More disturbing to our minds, this continuity is frequently punctuated by the fact that the kind, generous and saintly are sometimes visited by terrible deaths or afflictions.

We may have intimations that we are evolving inwardly, but we may also feel that we are constantly trying to navigate in the milieu of a slow, resistant, obstructive, and seemingly capricious world. If we are progressing toward some goal we have set for ourselves, then we need to know what cosmic Law speaks to our outer life, to seize upon something that can provide us with a palpable order and a map for our travel. Are we at the mercy of blind chance or some game of cosmic probability where you survive only if you are lucky? We should recall the firm counsel Sri Aurobindo gives us (full text on p. 44) that begins:

Chance, that shadow of an infinite possibility, must be banished from the dictionary of our perceptions; for of chance we can make nothing, because it is nothing. Chance does not at all exist; it is only a word by which we cover and excuse our own ignorance. [4-1]

Clearly, if there are universal laws governing the progress of the soul's evolution, the environment of that evolution must also have a corresponding universal order in the same way that biological evolution is worked out through the ecological principles and physical interactions in the grand theater of Nature. One of the most basic principles of ecology is the seamless integrality of all organisms with one another and with their encompassing physical environment, an integrality that moves unbroken through space and time and apparently has existed since the origin of the universe. [4-2] It is the orchestra that plays the ascending symphony of evolution. Its counterpart in the inner world is *karma.*

103

Fundamentally, the meaning of karma is that all existence is the working of a universal Energy, a process and an action and a building of things by that action, --- an unbuilding too, but as a step to farther building, --- that all is a continuous chain in which every one link is bound indissolubly to the past infinity of numberless links, and the whole governed by fixed relations, a fixed association of cause and effect, present action the result of past action as future action will be the result of present action, all cause a working of energy and all effect too a working of energy. [4-3]

It is immediately satisfying to our minds to know that Vedic wisdom encompasses *karma*'s integration with the evolutionary process and its interactions with rebirth, as part of our existence. What is not clear, even with this assurance, is how we make choices in our day-to-day lives given that not all of us are equally aware of an inner existence and of the laws governing us, and some may be completely ignorant or dismissive of them.

There are obviously many stages between stark unawareness and full awakening. Both Sri Chinmoy and Sri Aurobindo tell us that until we begin to have intimations of our souls' guidance, the Law of *Karma* is absolute and inescapable, merciless. We do evolve, but according to the slow pace of Nature, at *"the speed of an Indian bullock cart"* to use Sri Chinmoy's metaphor, and our current *karma* infallibly reflects our past actions. We may make the same kinds of mistakes life after life and have to suffer the results until we gradually discover our spiritual reality. Then our motives take their cues from our soul within, rather than from our vital and mental desires and expectations.

Karma as an instrument of the soul's evolution is unique to man, because of all living physical forms he alone has the attribute of *buddhi*, intelligent will, the potential to know, to choose and execute the will of the *purusha* (soul = *jivatman*) within, to develop the quality of *sattva*. In looking at the creation from bottom upwards, Sri Aurobindo comments,

*At the bottom are the existences in which tamas is supreme, the be-
ings who have not attained to the light of self-consciousness and are
utterly driven by the current of Nature. There is a will even in the
atom, but we see clearly enough that it is not free will, because it is
mechanical and the atom does not possess the will, but is possessed
by it. Next, in the plant the principle of rajas has struggled to the
surface, with its power of life, with its capacity of the nervous reac-
tions which in us are recognizable as pleasure and suffering, but
sattva is quite involved, has not yet emerged to awaken the light of a
conscious intelligent will; all is still mechanical, subconscient or half-
conscient, tamas stronger than rajas, both gaolers of the imprisoned
sattwa.*

*In the animal, though tamas is still strong, yet rajas prevails much
more against tamas, brings with it its developed power of life, desire,
emotion, passion, pleasure, suffering, while sattva, emerging, but
still dependent on the lower action, contributes to the first light of the
conscious mind, the mechanical sense of ego, conscious memory, a
certain kind of thought, especially the wonders of instinct and the
animal intuition. But as yet the buddhi, the intelligent will, has not
developed the full light of consciousness; therefore, no responsibility
can be attributed to the animal for its actions.* [4-4]

With humans, the rules undergo a profound change regarding action and karma, and Sri Aurobindo explains the apparently animal
propensities of our species,

*It is true that the principle of rajas or the principle of tamas gets hold
of his buddhi and induces it to justify any and every action he com-
mits or any avoidance of action; but still the justification or at least
the reference to the buddhi must be there either before or after the
action is committed. And, besides, in man sattva is awake and acts
not only as intelligence and intelligent will, but as a seeking for light,
for right knowledge and right action according to that knowledge, as
a sympathetic perception of the existence and claims of others, as an
attempt to know the higher law of his own nature, which the sattvic
principle in him creates, and to obey it, and as a conception of the*

greater peace and happiness which virtue, knowledge and sympathy bring in their train. He knows more or less imperfectly that he has to govern his rajasic and his tamasic by his sattvic nature and that thither tends the perfection of his normal humanity. [4-5]

There are three classes of *karma* that apply to human thought and action. With *sanchita karma*, many past actions have accumulated, including those done in previous lives, which have not yet borne fruit. Whereas, in *prarabdha karma* we get the experiences resulting from actions done in the distant past or in former lives, whether good or bad. If it is bad karma, then we suffer, and if it is good karma, then we enjoy it. With *agami karma* effects are worked out through the thoughts and actions performed by a fully awakened soul without expectation of reward and in complete harmony with the soul's or the Supreme Will and do not incur negative karmic results.

At this stage of human evolution, most of humanity is facing *sanchita karma*, accumulated karma which starts functioning as *prarabha karma*. There is no escape from this aspect of fate. It is like a devouring lion striking from the distant past, but when we get the results of *agami karma* the lion is roaring with divine victory and fulfillment in our life and all Earth gets the benefit. [4-6]

Although we are usually prone to focus on our own personal *karma*, the Law embraces all levels of human association, including thought, from individual through family, tribe, nation, international alliances and any other level of shared intent and assent to action. These karmic consequences affect all members of the group, even if some members were not in agreement with what the group leaders have said and done.

For large groups such as nations, the Law of Karma may use Mother Nature as the instrument through Earthquakes, volcanic eruptions, drought, violent storms, floods, or disease. The interactions are not confined just to relations within the human family but also our actions affecting the planetary environment, Mother Earth.

Clearly, we will need to discuss this topic more fully when we focus on environmental stewardship and service.

Seers of both ancient as well as modern times know that each human is most essentially a mental being. Although arising out of an animal lineage, he or she is destined to evolve beyond the limitations of the physical mind, the mind that is still largely immersed in *karma* entangled in and subservient to the workings of physical gratification, survival, striving for power, possessions and the vital instincts of procreation. The gravity of the Divine within us acting in and through the soul and heart must gradually but ineluctably pull the emotions and mind toward a higher vision's realization and purpose. Sri Chinmoy discusses the inner process.

> The dawning of the higher self within is the fruit of help from within or from a spiritual teacher in addition to practices such as prayer and meditation. Without these aides to experience the inner truth, progress is slow, arduous, and full of obstruction.
>
> Each soul comes into the world to do something special. Each soul is like a soldier. The divine soldier can achieve the utmost, fulfill the Supreme to the utmost, only when it has a commander-in-chief. If the soldier works under the direct guidance of the commander, then his mission on Earth is infinitely more successful, because the commander-in-chief can tell the soldier what is the right thing to do. If the individual soul wants to work, it will work like a tiny drop, with the capacity of a tiny drop. But if it works under the strict guidance of the commander-in-chief and with the assistance of all the forces at his command, then it will have the capacity of the entire ocean. The commander-in-chief is the Guru, who is in touch with the Absolute Supreme and represents the Absolute Supreme on Earth. Each individual soul sees it and realizes it according to the soul's own evolution.
>
> First the individual soul makes a promise to the Absolute Supreme that it will do something really good, divine, illumining and fulfilling. But in order to fulfill that promise it needs constant guidance,

encouragement, inspiration and help either directly from the Su-
preme or from the spiritual master who plays the role of the com-
mander-in-chief. 4-7

When you try to discover yourself, when you want to know what you
truly are, God's infinite Bounty dawns on you. With your self-dis-
covery, you can reveal God's Omniscience, Omnipotence and Omni-
presence here on Earth. It is here on Earth and nowhere else that God-
realization and God-manifestation can and will take place.

In order to be surcharged with will-power, we need concentration,
meditation and contemplation. We have to know how to concentrate.
When our concentration is perfect, we have to enter into meditation.
When our meditation is perfect, we have to enter into contemplation.
4-8

How can we learn to concentrate? Just by reading books? No, impos-
sible. Books will give us inspiration, nothing more. In order to learn
the secret of concentration, one has to go to a spiritual Teacher. 4-9

Many of us have not yet found a spiritual teacher or are not ready
to accept one, but still want to begin to add a spiritual dimension to
our lives. However, there are opportunities to learn the basics of concentration and meditation from the writings of and about the great
masters and from classes and advice given in many communities by
their students. Concentration, meditation, and contemplation are not
religious practices. They are simply techniques to learn about and experience the inner dimensions of oneself.

The Problem of Free Will Revisited

Most of us are not aware that we are evolving at every moment
of our existence, and it is perfectly natural that we should entertain
feelings that the Law of Karma leaves us bereft of free will. In the
West, free will is a cherished jewel of the personal liberties we all feel
we should enjoy. However, from Sri Chinmoy's or Sri Aurobindo's

yogic point of view, it is quite the opposite. What we actually are experiencing with our free will is mostly the karmic patterns, the *samskaras* of habitual responses, laid down for us by our vital and mental indulgences in this and past lives. It may also seem unjust that the universe should be operating on such a restrictive, deceptive and apparently punitive premise. Sri Aurobindo voices his impatience with this line of thought.

> *We suffer for our sins in another body; we shall be rewarded for our virtues in this; and so it will go on ad infinitum. No wonder, the philosophers found this a bad business and proposed as a remedy to get rid of both sin and virtue and even as our highest good to scramble anyhow out of a world so amazingly governed.*
>
> *Obviously, the scheme of things is only a variation of the old spiritual-material bribe and menace, the bribe of a Heaven of fat joys for the good and the threat of eternal fire or bestial tortures for the wicked. The idea of the Law of the world as primarily a dispenser of rewards and punishments is cognate to the idea of the Supreme Being as a judge, "father" and school-master, who is continually rewarding with lollipops his good boys and continually caning his naughty urchins. Man insists continually in making God in his own image instead of seeking to make himself more and more in the image of God, and all these ideas are the reflection of the child and the savage and the animal in us, which we have still failed to transform or outgrow. We should be inclined to wonder how these fancies of children found their way into such profound philosophical religions as Buddhism and Hinduism, if it were not so patent that men will not deny themselves the luxury of tacking on the rubbish from their past to the deeper thoughts of their sages.*[4-10]

On the other hand, individuality is not and cannot be lost. In Nature, individual species exist in the milieu of the universal evolutionary and ecological dance. They are shaped by all that surrounds them, and they in turn exert their specific influence on the larger general movement in which they are embedded. They are influenced by their heredity and the historical evolutionary current that has carried them along in time and space.

For humans, we must add the dimension of karmic consequence and the awakening *buddhi* to the current that carries us along, but it is clear that we need to fashion for ourselves a new individuality that fits our extended environment, a soul identity. Sri Aurobindo uses this imagery in relation to his own life.

> … *this brings in at once the whole necessity of past birth and karma. I am a persistent being who pursue my evolution within the persistent being of the world. I have evolved my human birth and I help constantly in the human evolution. I have created by my past karma my own conditions and my relations with others and the general karma. That shapes my heredity, my environment, my affinities, my connections, my material, my opportunities and obstacles, a part of my predestined powers and results, not arbitrarily predestined but predetermined by my own stage of nature and past action, and on this groundwork I build new karma and farther strengthen or subtilize my power of natural being, enlarge my experience, go on with my soul evolution. This process is woven in with the universal evolution and all its lines are included in the web of being, but it is not merely a jutting point or moment of it or a brief tag shot into the tissue. That is what rebirth means in the history of my manifested self and of universal being.* [4-11]

Lifting the Karmic Debt

In the Bhagavad Gita, Krishna tells Arjuna,

> *Whenever unrighteousness is on the ascendant and righteousness is on the decline, I body Myself forth. To protect and preserve the virtuous and put an end to the evil-doers, to establish dharma, I manifest Myself from age to age.* [4-12]

Krishna declares himself an *avatar*, an incarnation of the Absolute Supreme (Lord Vishnu). Sri Chinmoy has said on many occasions that the *avatars* and great realized souls come to Earth specifically to help the aspiring souls to progress and to kindle the flame of aspiration in those who have yet to discover it within themselves. These appearances are critically timed to coincide with periods of stress, when humanity needs divine help to make a forward leap of consciousness.

This is God's promise and compassion for humanity, and the compassion shown by the great masters can take the form of nullifying negative karma or taking it upon themselves to relieve our suffering. Even if a master is not on Earth, an aspirant can invoke his presence and ask forgiveness for past mistakes or for his karma to be remitted. We should not forget that Creator and creation are inseparable in Indian spiritual wisdom, and as a mother has complete identification and oneness-love for her child, the same is true of the Creator for his creations, humanity and the Earth. Although no one escapes the sting of karma during the soul's evolution, Sri Chinmoy emphasizes the positive effects of suffering for our mistakes.

> *It is for the sake of the soul's growth that karma exists.*[4-13] *The Law of Karma does not actually bind the soul; through karma the soul gets experiences.*[4-14] *It is enriched by all the experiences which the personality derives through the Laws of Karma.* [4-15] *God's compassion always and always overrides the law of karma. Had it been otherwise, no human being on Earth could have lasted even for a single day.* [4-16] *This experience is necessary, because through it a new wisdom dawns in the person's consciousness.* [4-17] *The Law of Karma itself is another form of God's compassion. You may call it blessingful love in disguise.* [4-18]

With our attainment of some inner wisdom also comes the necessity and the capacity of a self-discipline that allows our wisdom and power to enter into the physical and vital energies, which are essential to our life on Earth, but that gives over them our control and guidance. Their transformation under the guidance of our higher nature will bring a creative dynamism to the egoistic demands of the vital, and even the physical body will gradually become conscious of its purposes in service to the *jivatman* within.

With practice, we can learn to invoke and to experience the radiance native to our being. This gradually leads us to the truth that we are instruments of a higher Force and can participate in a vastly expanded arena of play. The lines the first stanza of Sri Chinmoy's poem, *The Absolute* (Chapter 1,), strike our consciousness with a new depth,

> *No mind, no form, I only exist*
> *Now ceased all will and thought*
> *The final end of Nature's dance*
> *I am it whom I have sought.*

It is in this understanding that our relationship to *karma* begins to change, and the fixity of our karmic fate takes on mutable hues. The seeds of *agami karma* are sown.

> *The easiest and most effective way of freeing yourself from the bonds of karma is to feel that you are not the doer. You are just an instrument. An instrument is not responsible, but the Doer, who is the Supreme, is responsible. If one can feel all the time that there is Somebody else who is the Doer and he is merely the instrument, then who will be responsible? The Doer. If He does something wrong, He is responsible; if He does something good then He will be appreciated. Unfortunately, in the ordinary life, it is impossible for the average human being to think that he is not the doer. If he does something wrong then he curses himself and says, "I made a mistake." If on the other hand he does something right, he is bloated with pride and feels that he alone did it. Our human action compels us to feel that we deserve the fruit. But if we feel that we are not the doer, the result goes to the One who has actually acted.* 4-19

By approaching the Source, which embodies both action and the Doer, *karma* may be changed or even nullified. However, even if we still have *karma* to work out from past acts in this or previous lives, we try to take a much wiser approach to the experiences we encounter. There is an old saying that *"Experiences that do not kill us make us stronger."* When an obstacle or misfortune stands in our way, we need to ask ourselves, "What can I learn from this? Perhaps this is an opportunity to overcome fear, insecurity, pride, doubt or other negative qualities that dog my life." In this case, we see *karma* not as a punishment but an opportunity to expand, learn and grow.

One of the tools we can use to understand our own karma and the various cosmic forces that affect our soul's progress toward greater illumination is the Indian system of astrology known as *jyotish*. Whatever we may think of popular contemporary Western astrology and astrologers, astrological knowledge has been a foundation of nearly every ancient civilization: China, Egypt, Greece, Babylonia and India as well as the American Mayan and Incan cultures. *Jyotish* or the *Bhrigu* system (the Sanskrit word *jyotish* means inner illumination) is rooted in Vedic wisdom, especially in its acknowledgement that the universe is bound together as a single bond of light and love.

A subset of this wisdom is the rapidly growing body of ecological thinking that sees the whole planet as a single functioning being in which all forms are integrally interdependent in all levels of conscious existence. Vedic astrology is the expansion of this thought to include the whole cosmos. The stars, planets and their presiding *devas* have life and consciousness, influencing us in many subtle ways. As such, *jyotish* is a sacred practice. At one time *jyotish* was an inseparable part of ayurvedic medicine [4-20], and today it is used by many healers as a reliable means to determine if health imbalances have karmic origins. It also aids diagnoses at the level of the cosmic unity to which we are joined, and which contributes to the karmic flow and harmony of all other levels of our life: physical, vital, mental and psychic.

We will discuss the science of Ayurveda in greater detail in the final chapter.

However, if we take up the spiritual life to aspire for higher truth or are fortunate to have the guidance of a realized master, even the *jyotish* horoscopes are not accurate. If we seek inner Light, we can change or transcend our karmic fate. Although Sri Chinmoy on several occasions praised the precision of the *jyotish* astrology, when he was still a child in Bengal, he had his horoscope read. The astrologer told Sri Chinmoy's family that he could not see anything beyond the child's thirteenth birthday. It was in his thirteenth year that he achieved full realization.

Notes on Chapter 4

4-1.   Sri Aurobindo. 1991. *Rebirth and Karma.* p. 71. Lotus Light Publ., Wilmot, WI

4-2.   Swimme, B.T. and M.E. Tucker. 2011. *Journey of the Universe.* xi + 175 pp. Yale Univ. Press, New Haven, CT. This book is a remarkable telescoping of the scientific version of the creation of the universe from the "big bang" to the present. It acknowledges the continuous and ubiquitous operation of evolutionary and ecological processes throughout.

4-3.   Sri Aurobindo. 1991. *Rebirth and Karma.* p. 69. Lotus Light Publ., Wilmot, WI

4-4.   Sri Aurobindo. 1997. *Essays on the Gita.* pp. 218-219. Sri Aurobindo Ashram, Pondicherry, India.

4-5.   Ibid. pp. 220-221.

4-6.   Sri Chinmoy. 1976. *Sri Chinmoy Speaks, Part 9.* Pp. 23-29. Agni Press, Jamaica, N.Y.

4-7.   Sri Chinmoy. 2015. *Victory to My Supreme.* pp. 125-126. Perfection-Glory Press, Augsburg, Germany.

4-8.   Ibid. pp. 127-128.

4-9.   Sri Chinmoy. 1973. *Eastern Light for the Western Mind.* pp. 99-102. Aum Publ., Jamaica, N.Y.

4-10. Sri Aurobindo. 1991. *Rebirth and Karma.* pp 8-9. Lotus Light Publ., Wilmot, WI.

4-11. Ibid. p. 99.

4-12. Sri Chinmoy. 1996. *Commentaries on the Vedas, the Upanishads and the Bhagavad Gita.* pp. 169-170. Aum Publ., Jamaica, N.Y.

4-13. Sri Chinmoy. 1974. *Yoga and the Spiritual Life.* p. 126. Agni Press, Jamaica, N.Y.

4-14. Sri Chinmoy. 1976. *The Soul's Evolution.* pp. 10-14. Agni Press, Jamaica, N.Y.

4-15. Sri Chinmoy. 1974. *Yoga and the Spiritual Life.* p. 126. Agni Press, Jamaica, N.Y.

4-16. Sri Chinmoy. 1978. *Service Heroes.* Agni Press, Jamaica, N.Y.

4-17. Sri Chinmoy. 1974. *Death and Reincarnation.* pp. 109-113. Agni Press, Jamaica, N.Y.

4-18. Sri Chinmoy. 1978. *Service Heroes.* Agni Press, Jamaica, N.Y.

4-19. Sri Chinmoy. 1978. *Earth's Cry Meets Heaven's Smile, Book 3.* p. 34. Aum Press, Santurce, Puerto Rico.

4-20. For an excellent and detailed presentation of the *Jyotish* system of astrology, see Frawley, David. 2005, *Ayurvedic Astrology: Self-Healing Through the Stars.* Motilal Banarsidass Publ., Delhi, India.

DHARMA & RADIANT DEEDS

Karma & Dharma

K*arma* and *Dharma* rhyme, and in the universal scheme of things they are closely linked in the unfolding evolutionary drama of humanity. *Karma* is the voice of all our deeds and thoughts in the universal music, and *dharma* reflects the conscious harmonization of our deeds and thoughts according to our soul's will and trajectory of progress. Both Sri Chinmoy and Sri Aurobindo respectively (below) make this clear in their constant urgings to aim only at the highest attainment, full realization, however long it may take.

Dharma is God-invocation and God-acceptance in God's own Way. Victory is life-perfection and self-transcendence. [5-1]

We must then, in order to understand the Gita's description of the work of the Avatar, take the idea of the Dharma, in its fullest, deepest and largest conception, as the inner and outer law by which the divine Will and Wisdom work out the spiritual evolution of mankind and its circumstances and results in the life of the race. Dharma in the Indian conception is not merely the good, the right, morality and justice, ethics; it is the whole government of all the relations of man with other beings, with Nature, with God, considered from the point of view of a divine principle working itself out in forms and laws of action, forms of the inner and the outer life, orderings of every kind in the world. [5-2]

It is clear in the *Vishnu Purana* [5-3] that the creation of our world (Mother Earth = *Prithivi*) provided a paradise of beauty, diversity and harmony as the theater for the evolution of spiritual Truth in and through humanity. All the realms of higher and lower consciousness, social structure, biodiversity, climates, seas, mountains, fertile soil, scriptures (the Vedas) rituals for constant grounding of the mind in the divine origin of things, and the ever-present *Dharma* for life, as voiced anew by contemporaries Sri Chinmoy and Sri Aurobindo, were inseparably bound together from the very beginning.

Acknowledging that the rulers of the first human clans (*e.g.* Manu [5-4]) were imperfect beings evolving out of *tamasic* and *rajasic* roots toward *sattvic* life, yogis of deep spiritual wisdom, living exemplars of Vedic ideals and who conversed with higher beings, acted as advisors to these rulers. These masters safeguarded and perpetuated *Dharma*, despite the vital propensities of their charges.

To act against *Dharma* was to invite calamity and strife in the kingdom, for we must remember that Vishnu also endowed the Earth-creation not only with pathways to progress and divinity, but also with the weaknesses, deflections, temptations and the asuric beings who preside over these qualities in the inner worlds. The balancing power of karma made sure that transgressions would be revisited later in evolutionary life but with the opportunity to transform them and move upward.

The epic struggles portrayed in the *Ramayana* and the *Mahabharata* (in which the *Bhagavad Gita* is one chapter) tell of the work of two great avatars, King Rama and Krishna. Both Rama and Krishna are incarnations of the Vishnu himself, come to Earth to return the rule of *Dharma* when the power of the asuric forces (*adharma*) had crossed the line and become intolerable for the progress of the world. Besides revealing the initial stages of creation, the *Vishnu Purana* describes each of the avatars of Vishnu that descended, in accordance with his Promise, when the ignorance forces had become predominant. The hope of humanity and the Promise of the Creator are deeply embedded in the life of India, despite the sometimes-rough seas of current events.

As spiritual masters, Sri Chinmoy and Sri Aurobindo have taught their students that spiritual progress is movement in thought and deed toward the goal of realization, and any condition not directed toward that goal, that does not open the consciousness to the inner Will, is outside the flow of one's life-*dharma*, a deflection or a step backwards. On the other hand, both compassionately devote the great preponderance of their writings to the fact that humanity as a whole is on a gradual journey toward spiritual perfection, and that a universal practical *dharma* is not yet fixed and can relate only to whatever level of consciousness a person or group currently manifests.

Here is a simple and practical example. Someone takes a daily run of two miles to maintain his fitness. He has friends who have trained for many weeks or months and have completed marathons. He takes up the challenge to go beyond his present capacity and aspires to run 26.2 miles but worries that he may be hampered by some past injuries or not have the time for the necessary training.

A fitness coach suggests he start slowly by making his daily run 2.5 miles and then work up to three or four miles, to concentrate on the moment-by-moment preparations to condition his body: stretching, diet, frame of mind, adequate sleep, proper running clothes and shoes. He begins by buying new running shoes and making the first of the increments in his distance. His *svadharma* (personal *dharma)* will the disciplines necessary to get to three miles a day, then to four, five, eight, ten and finally to 26.2. The *svadharma* is changing, but not the goal or the source of his determination and effort.

If he attains victory in this self-transcendent battle with his body's lethargic demands, he will doubtless be inspired to work on other personal habits that impede his progress toward integral perfection and happiness. The discipline and experience of completing the marathon will strengthen his self-confidence and carry over to new goals and activities. It will also positively transform his image and interactions with others and add to his own good karma.

Personal transformation and world transformation are inseparable. When one person raises his consciousness by transcending physical, vital and mental limitations his *svadharma* changes, and that changes the milieu of the planetary *dharma*. True, the world will slowly and eventually evolve and progress by fits and starts; but when individuals or groups make conscious effort to deepen their awareness, the consequences affect not only their personal spiritual progress but also that of everyone. Everything ascends and accelerates.

The following discussions will concentrate on the changing *dharma* of three broad current concerns, ethics, environment and medicine. My purpose is to elucidate in a very general sense how Indian spiritual wisdom can inspire and guide future solutions and actions while drawing attention to growing bodies of consensus that already embody and manifest spiritual values. I have explored this process from a different perspective with other examples in *Light, Truth and Nature*.[5-5]

Dharma & Ethics

Yogic ethics take their base in experiencing the unity of Creator and creation, of the individual and the universal. Therefore, the issue of inclusiveness never arises. The Supreme consciousness is in all. All have value. Nothing is excluded. For a fully realized master, there is no need for ethics, only the automatic obedience to the Will coming from within. The yogi is the embodiment of the ultimate *dharma* as described by Sri Chinmoy and Sri Aurobindo on pp. 127-128.

The necessity of ethical standards arises because nearly everyone belongs to the community of evolving humanity in which some souls are older and more spiritually aware than others. With spiritual growth, the sphere of our *svadharma*, our personal identity and thus ethics expands. The devil is in the details of trying to negotiate a higher standard for human behavior and intent within a global society that currently has strongly divergent views about what those standards and intentions should be.

In these discussions, *Dharma* is a term preferable to *ethics* because the former implicitly acknowledges the Truth of the Creator as the Source guiding every aspect of planetary evolution. In the language of conventional ethical dialogue, we currently seek a standard of normative behavior among planetary stakeholders, *all* of whom feel they *are* normative.

Unfortunately, it is often true that when such debates take place, it appears fair to give all sides equal weight, time and hearing, but by using this tactic, ignorance and illumination, *dharma* and *adharma*, the Pandavas and the Kauravas, will deserve equal consideration or potential value. This is an approach that appeals to and emboldens the lower levels of human consciousness, a compromise mixing muddied water with pure and serving it up for all to drink. It is an unfortunate misapplication of democratic principles, but one that is perhaps unavoidable if no one in the arena is able to recognize, champion and lead toward a higher spiritual standard.

Guidance for human leadership needs to come from the more illumined *sattvic* quarter, not from whatever *rajasically* driven individuals or groups have the loudest voice, most aggressive military power and deepest pockets.

This is why in Vedic India sages were always given the role of advising kings and emperors and why many tribal governments were (and still are) advised by groups of the wisest elders. The rishis and elders counselling their rulers were not so much acting as a physical check on misguided action as they were providing firm but compassionate wisdom. They knew and identified with the power of vital emotions and desires because in their own *sadhana* they had tamed them in themselves. Moreover, royal families as well as ordinary citizens had been educated to respect and value the *dharma* anchoring their society. It is from the leaders with inner vision we have gotten the United Nations, the Universal Declaration of Human Rights, The Earth Charter, and the principles of sustainable development.

With spiritual awakening comes the power of inner discrimination. The heart-Light, in unison with the soul, provides intrinsic and infallible guidance to separate divisive and egoistic promptings of the lower *chakras* from the vision of the Creator trying to inform our thought and action.

Using the yogic perspective as an Everest of standards, the wiser among us will always firmly but lovingly steer toward governance and acts that are more supportive and inclusive, not only of the well-being of all humans but also of the entire Earth-creation: non-human life and the physical environment in all its diversity. Such ethics will evoke a *dharma* more focused on the Earth as a shared *community of life* and less upon destructive and competitively divisive economic, political, socio-cultural, and religious perspectives.

To be successful in building a global consensus, there must come a concomitant frame-shift of emphasis at every level of educational systems that disciplines and steers the mind toward the intrinsic truth and value of these principles and encourages the dynamic aspect of the vital with rigor and cheerfulness.

As discussed in Chapter 1, this is one of the great issues in scientific and especially environmental ethics, where there is a struggle to promote a vision, a *dharma* of humanity in the context of Earth in which we are all valued and all have responsibilities.

The following simply arranged table [5-6] can help us see where we have to go both in the individual and group dynamic to achieve a planetary *dharma*. At the moment many of us are stuck somewhere between levels 3 and 5, which are within the domain of the vital and lower levels of mind.

```
9. Transcendental (Yogic)
8. Universe
7. Life-Planet
6. Humanity
5. Race/Culture/Religion
4. Nation
3. Tribe
2. Family
1. Individual
```

It is greatly encouraging though that there are literally hundreds, perhaps thousands of organizations, springing up like mushrooms, ranging from neighborhood initiatives to the United Nations Sustainable Development Goals, dedicated to raising us to a firm purchase at level 6. From there ecological thinking and the waxing Light of the global heart *chakra* will eventually raise us up in confidence to grasp the seventh rung and envision the rungs above.

Environment & Spirituality:
Setting the Stage for Transformation

Humanity is currently struggling to rediscover and transform its integral relationship with Mother Earth. The primary term of the relationship has never changed, our spiritual connection, originating in the creation of the universe and in the progressing evolution of life. Millennia of yogic experience extending from the time of the Vedas and *Vishnu Purana*, through the *Bhagavad Gita* to the vision of contemporaries Sri Chinmoy and Sri Aurobindo affirm that in the inner world, man and Mother Earth are one in essential being. Creator and creation are inseparable, united in the hallowed bond of love divine.

Even the knowledge of science, based as it is in the intellectual mind and physical senses, confirms the existence of an unbroken flow of events and purposeful relationships from the "big bang" to the immediate present tense of universal evolution. [5-7] Integrality of evolutionary and ecological thought assuredly tells us that humankind is indissolubly bound into the cycles and balances of nature, that there can be no separate existence for us outside the obligations of our participation in the environmental dance of life. The expansion of human intellectuality to a universal scope is in itself part of the irreversible spiritual unfolding of the soul-force within.

Despite the vastness of our understanding of our place in the cosmos and even in the minutiae of the quotidian movements in our local habitations, we find ourselves in the midst of doing terrible damage to the global environment. Consequently, we find ourselves plunged into the throes of a wrenching suffering. If we have some inner awareness of the Earth consciousness, the pain of the outer damage, what we feel and see personally, is a reflection and consequence of the inner suffering felt at every level of being contained within Mother Earth.

We ask how the vision and the reality can be so out of joint. As a species we are sitting like Arjuna in his chariot poised on the field of Kurukshetra looking to our charioteer to pilot us into battle and elicit actions to save us from our own ignorance and weakness. In Arjuna's time, the yogis (*e.g.* Krishna and contemporary sages) fully experienced and understood the spiritual dynamics of creation's evolution; but there was no shared intellectual concept of "globalism" or of our physical origins in the vast cosmic drama that science has brought into focus in our own time.

In 1984, Sri Chinmoy was invited to a local New York television station's program, *The First Estate,* to discuss a spiritual approach to impending nuclear warfare. Although the topic of the program 35 years ago was a possible nuclear holocaust, Sri Chinmoy's comments could as well apply to the environmental crises of today. The host, Dr. Russell Barber, asked, "Well, Sri Chinmoy, are we going to blow ourselves all up?" The answer came without hesitation.

No, because the world does not belong to us. Out of his infinite bounty, God has created this world. God is the Creator and we are the creation. The Creator has infinitely more power than the creation. He will never allow us to destroy the world, no matter how hard we try. I have that abiding faith from within. People talk about war and destruction, but I feel that deep within their heart of hearts, they feel the necessity of having inner peace. They know that by destroying others [i.e. the planetary environment] they will never have peace.[5-8]

This is the crux of the matter; the world does not belong to us. Quite the reverse, from the inner perspective we belong to the world. In the present stage of human evolution, a large portion of humanity is, to a greater or lesser degree, still controlled by the vital and lower mental consciousness that desires personal or tribal/national power, material wealth, superiority and recognition. While this condition is appropriate to the animal world, which, as Sri Aurobindo points out, has no karmic liability for its actions, as humans we do have an intrinsic if veiled conscious access to our spiritual source. We do have responsibility for what we do to the planetary environment. While we may appear deaf to the cries and pangs of the Earth and her myriad creatures, at a deeper level we are aware of that pain and disharmony we create, and with that awareness comes karmic consequence.

In 1978, I was fortunate to attend one of Sri Chinmoy's public meditations in New York City. I was then a neophyte in the world of meditation, in the early stages of developing a regular practice. After the meditation, he called for questions from the audience, and I raised my hand and asked, "What is the supreme goal of science?" He smiled, paused a moment and replied, "You are a biologist. In your case, you must learn to see life in everything, not just in plants and animals. Everything in the universe has life." At the time, I was grappling with integrating what I knew about the world as a scientist and what I was learning from my own meditation. It was an epiphany, after which my extensive experience working in natural environments quite literally took on new light. My *svadharma* had changed.

124

We begin to recognize the arrogance of our view of Earth as primarily a Natural Resource to be used, rather than an Intimate Presence to evoke that wonder and beauty, that healing and inspiration that is the fulfillment of our inner world. The natural world does indeed feed, clothe and shelter us physically. Yet if we look to Earth simply as a resource to be exploited for its monetary value as well as for our human comfort and convenience, we will end up with a planet severely damaged in its life-giving capacities.

We need to understand that Earth in its primordial condition nourishes us in our inner spirit even while it provides for our physical needs. 5-9

This passage by Thomas Berry could only have been written after he himself had an epiphany about his personal connection to the Earth and the universe. He describes that his moment of clarity came when he was standing in a meadow near his home in North Carolina. He saw and felt the Creator's Light inside the creation, the beauty, balances, cycles and his own life's true value, meaning, fulfillment and work.

Things have fallen out of balance. Scientific knowledge about the environment is not enough. Intellectual understanding and technology are not enough. These achievements, unguided by light of the soul, can and have frequently fallen under the dominion of the desire-bound *rajasic* nature of the vital and physical mind. The results are everywhere: struggles for supremacy, power and wealth; a view that the Earth is nothing more than a supply depot for natural resources. The corollary of this view is the devaluation of beauty and of life. The capstone and jewel of our inner wisdom, the *sattvic* spiritual heart, needs to be awakened, heeded and strengthened.

Coming back to the plight of Arjuna, central to the meaning of the *Bhagavad Gita*, each of us with our personal immortal *buddhic* connection to inner Truth, is crying consciously or unconsciously for guidance and illumination. We each have a high purpose through which we will be empowered, despite our cloying insecurity and feeling of powerlessness. We may not be so fortunate to have the physical presence of someone like Krishna driving our life-chariot, but we all have access to the yoga of *awakening and action*. This is the radiant yoga which has been passed down the ages from the Creator to the gods to the Vedic sages and from sage to sage undiluted down the millennia to the sages of the present day.

Awakening is absolutely necessary. It is in fact guaranteed in the process of evolution and reincarnation, but even that is not enough. To solve the enigma of our 21st. century identity crisis, the awakening needs to be *consciously sought* and then translated into radiant actions, which take their energy and dedication in the light of awakening. For Arjuna, his *svadharma* was to go into battle as a surrendered, detached instrument of Lord Krishna. Once we make the connection, our path will be made clear by our karma and our soul's mission.

Awakening to Nature

With the emphasis of *awakening* our innate connection to Mother Earth and universal Nature, there are many gateways of experience open to us, although some are in need of repair and redesigning.

1. Evolution

We can wait indefinitely for the hour when the connection reappears on its own, but that means that we will continue to be the instruments of the vital and lower mind and contribute more to problems than solutions. Safe and sure, but not a path for those who feel any sense of duty or urgency.

2. Experience of Unspoiled Nature

Universal Nature herself is a bountiful source of inspiration and awakening.

For many years when I was teaching ecology and sustainability at the university level, one of the first exercises I did with my students was to ask them a simple question, in the form of an anonymous "educational survey." I asked them briefly to list the five most important things they received from whatever they conceived to be "Nature."

75-80% of the several thousands of responses were physical provisions: water, energy, heat, food, materials, etc. The remaining 20-25% were intangible, more subtle qualities. The top two in the latter category were beauty and peace (often couched in words such "stress relief" or "freedom from anxiety"). Some of the many other qualities cited frequently included inspiration, spiritual oneness and belonging, gratitude, happiness, renewal, freedom, creative insight, and love. I shared the results with the class and discussed how their own feelings might guide their actions as participants in the world environmental arena.

In another "educational survey" I used several times in both science and non-science classes, involved students writing down whatever physical characteristics "paradise" should have if they were given a ticket to travel there personally. While with only several dozen responses as opposed to several thousand in the previous survey, there was a strikingly clear pattern. The great majority of the responses were qualities aesthetically tied to Earth's environment: mountains, seas, rivers, flowers, breezes, birds, sunsets and sunrises, forests, pleasant temperatures. Only a handful listed items like shopping malls, technology or good finances.

From whatever past life experiences, I was a born entomologist. I wanted to catch butterflies starting from the time I could walk independently around our property in rural North Carolina. I remember looking up at the tiger swallowtails hovering in place, as nearly all swallowtails do, taking nectar from lilac blossoms several feet above my head. For me they were the ultimate beauty, but out of reach. I can still feel the joy that attended my first capture, which I achieved by bending the lilac stem down *cum* feeding butterfly and grabbing it in mid-meal.

When I brought the struggling insect inside to my parents, they were amazed that I had managed to catch it, and then immediately instructed me how to hold it without damaging its wings. Over ensuing years, they taught me how to identify and preserve the specimens I caught, learn their ecological requirements and to plant "butterfly gardens" on our property to attract local species with the right larval host plants and nectar-producing flowers. A career was born.

Not every child is as fortunate. Many urban children have little or no contact with the natural environment, obstructing the door to self-knowledge and the awakening of our universal consciousness-connections. In 2006, a book appeared by Richard Louv, [5-10] an investigative journalist from California, LAST CHILD IN THE WOODS.

At the time, I was teaching an upper division course at Florida International University for juniors, seniors and graduate students, *Environmental Education Workshop*. One of the graduate students lent me Louv's book and wanted to know what I thought about it. I went through it over the next couple of days and returned it, thanking her sincerely. After that, it was required reading in the course, and parts of it found their way into my *Deep Ecology* course as well.

In my opinion, Louv's work is a companion in stature for its power of social awakening and factual basis to Rachel Carson's (1962) SILENT SPRING, [5-11] published more than 40 years before, and to Nicholas Carr's THE SHALLOWS *(What the Internet is Doing to our Brains)*. [5-12] The thesis of LAST CHILD IN THE WOODS is very simple. It describes how modern techno-urban culture is driving a wedge between the young and the direct experience of Nature.

The wedge has many components, and some of the major ones are:

- The destruction of natural wild habitats and the extirpation of wildlife populations in urban areas and their replacement by "sanitized" urban landscapes.

- The pervasive mental addiction to internet, social media, and video games in even very young children.

- A generation of parents and teachers who lack personal contact with Nature and are passing on to their children an intellectualized often fearful version of direct experience and exploration of what is perceived by them as a dangerous, dirty, unpleasant environment.

- Loss of opportunity for unstructured play in natural wild areas.

- A disconnection between the sources of food production and what ends up on the table.

- A blurring of the origins and boundaries of humans, animals and machines.

One of the great voices resounding throughout the world in the cause of ecological thinking, conservation and preservation is Edward O. Wilson, Pellegrino Professor emeritus of Zoology at Harvard University. I met him briefly when he visited his long-time friend and my doctoral thesis advisor, Prof. Thomas Eisner, at Cornell University in the 1960s. At the time, Wilson was eagerly pursuing studies of how ants integrated their colony activities through the use of pheromones (chemical cues used to communicate between members of the same species).

In the intervening years, Wilson's vision has vastly expanded. He has not only become an authority on sociobiology but has widened his concern to embrace the society of humans and its relationship to Mother earth, which he has examined in his more than 20 published books. Always proceeding from the foundations of ecological and evolutionary science, he has reached out to the general reader with complete sincerity and great depth of feeling promoting not only conservation, but a global, sustainable environmental ethic based on practical necessity, love of earth's beauty and self-discovery.

His concept of *biophilia* [5-13] is simply another way of expressing the oneness-love of Creator and creation, something he has inwardly experienced through his decades spent in the wild places of the world. Of *biophilia*, he has written,

Biophilia is the innate tendency to focus on life and lifelike processes.
To the degree that we come to understand other organisms, we will
place greater value on them and on ourselves.

For those seeking a bridge between science and spirituality, between human existence and the global environment, Wilson's life and writings are a good place to start. Here is more proof of the fact that spirituality does not negate science. It only adds greater love, compassion, clarity, humility, and power.

3. Prayer, Concentration & Meditation.

With regular practice, the physical mind and intellectual processes become quiet, and we can experience the deeper aspects of our being, especially the Light of the *heart chakra*, often completely veiled by mental and emotional turbidity. Access to nature's beauty can expedite our practice, but any quiet space will serve. If one is drawn to one of the realized masters, whether living or historical, concentration and invocation of that Presence and consciousness is of inestimable value. With the Light comes guidance, intuitive perception of the direction and tasks appropriate for your life will come forward from the soul within.

In my conversations with many meditator-friends over the decades, one of the first intimations of *sattvic* consciousness is often peace of mind, a breath of happiness and a sense of limitless possibilities. Following these openings will come the spiritual connection of all human beings to one another (level 6, p. 133). Further expansion of vision reveals the connection to Mother Earth and the universe (levels 7 and 8), and, once again, with expansion comes the increasingly clear voice of Inner Guidance.

4. Contact with Indigenous People

Humanity's most ancient form of spirituality is the land and environmentally-based practices of virtually all indigenous cultures. In

130

many nations, local Native brothers and sisters are offering programs, rituals and experiences, which spring from millennia of continuous immersion in the consciousness of Mother Earth. The language and ritual acts of native peoples are celebrations of what the yogis call the *eternal now*, the creation's omnipresence in ourselves and in universal Nature. They embody what Joseph Campbell calls *affect symbols* [5-14], images and actions that, like Sanskrit mantras, take us out of our ordinary consciousness and plunge us into the life of the inner reality.

After centuries of persecution and horrific suffering at the hands of modern nation-states whose technological superiority and religious and cultural intolerance has pushed many tribes to the brink of extinction, indigenous peoples are increasingly being recognized and valued as exemplars and teachers of environmental stewardship and sustainable living, which they actually have been for countless generations.

Colonialist Western empires and governments need not only beg forgiveness from those they have wronged so despicably, but also reverse and formally repudiate the policies of exploitation and marginalization they have embraced for many centuries. A rapprochement is possible, if for no other reason than our shared humanity, but the offending states will necessarily be under watchful scrutiny for many years depending on their sincerity and commitment to the healing process.

The indigenous inner perspective offers two priceless gifts to other members of the human family. First, they offer millennia-old spiritual bonds and rituals invoking their ancestors, deities of local and regional environments and the spirit of universal creation. Here is an accessible path to knowing and feeling the sacredness of all lands.

The second gift is one of healing. Out of ignorance, not only have we damaged and wounded the outer body of Mother Earth, but we have also diminished her inner divinity. The recovery of our awareness of the sacred nature of Earth is an indispensable step toward the healing of those wounds.

As I write this, several of my close friends are travelling to many sites around the world to help local native activists in their struggles against mining, drilling, deforestation, corporate agriculture, pollution and desecration of sacred lands. They have been threatened, and some have suffered serious injury and even death in remote areas where their campaigns have taken them. It is their feeling that radiant actions on behalf of Earth are worth this risk and supreme sacrifice.

5. Music, Poetry, & Other Arts

Sri Aurobindo is here addressing Indian educators, but is clearly indicating a universal integral Truth when he says,

> *Poetry raises the emotions and gives each its separate delight. Art stills the emotions and teaches them the delight of a restrained and limited satisfaction. Music deepens the emotions and harmonizes them with each other. Between them music, art and poetry are a perfect education for the soul; they make and keep its movements purified, deep and harmonious. These, therefore, are agents which cannot profitably be neglected by humanity on its onward march or degraded to the mere satisfaction of sensuous pleasure which will disintegrate rather than build the character. They are, when properly used, great educating, edifying and civilizing forces.* 5-15

Reflecting on the intrinsic union of Creator and creation, of Creator and man, and the built-in inner urge to aspire, evolve, ascend, and transcend ourselves in all aspects of life, he continues,

> *Shakti, Force, pouring through the universe supports its boundless activities, the frail and tremulous life of the rose no less than the flaming motions of sun and star.*

To suggest the strength and virile unconquerable force of the divine Nature in man and in the outside world, its energy, its calm, its powerful inspiration, its august enthusiasm, its wildness, its greatness, attractiveness, to breathe that into man's soul and gradually mold the finite into the image of the Infinite is another spiritual utility of Art. This is its loftiest function, its fullest consummation, its most perfect privilege. [5-16]

From the Mother's Perspective

In response to questions about the Earth's soul and environmental damage, Sri Chinmoy answered,

The Earth represents the Mother aspect of the Divine. It is on Earth that matter and spirit will find their absolute fulfillment through their reciprocal help and complete union. Matter will see through the eye of the spirit's vision. Spirit will flower and awaken by energizing Matter to become a perfect basis of physical immortality and human transformation on Earth. The two main characteristics of the soul of the Earth are aspiration and compassionate tolerance. [5-17]

Like all mothers, the Earth suffers from the ignorant activities of her children, and she feels pain and suffers damage when we lose our connection to her and act out of selfishness, violence, and greed.

In a moment of candor in 1990, Sri Chinmoy made the following revealing remarks to a gathering of his students in New York. This is the unique power of the realized yogi who has at his command the intimacy of an Earth-child with his Earth-Mother. As such, he represents us all, in this case almost as eavesdroppers on a sacred event.

The very nature of Earth is to cry, cry for purification. First it starts with a cry for simplicity, because the Earth has been polluted by complexity. Previously, hundreds and thousands of years ago, Earth was very simple. Now human beings have corrupted the Earth. On the one hand, machinery and technology have helped the Earth considerably, but on the other hand, they have considerably taken away the pristine beauty, purity, and divinity of Mother Earth. As soon as I

133

see the soul of the Earth, I see the soul is crying and crying because of the loss of its inner divinity, which is far, far greater than the gain in outer achievements. Earth has lost many, many divine qualities which it had from the beginning of creation. Earth was also tempted in the beginning to seek the new, the development of science, the development of the mental faculties, of the mind's capacities. Then the Earth saw, to its extreme sorrow, that although these developments definitely helped a little, many extremely, extremely beautiful qualities of Earth were being lost, allowing the outer achievements to dominate the inner life.

The very nature of Mother Earth is to cry. One kind of cry is aspiring to become one with God the Creator. But at the same time the Earth has another cry which is to regain the invaluable things it has lost over the centuries. [5-18]

Hopeful Signs.

There are many hopeful signs that a higher environmental *dharma* is slowly emerging, one that perhaps will restore to Earth some of her desecrated beauty. Although this emergence is not without widespread resistance, it is encouraging that it is arising simultaneously from diverse places in the human cultural landscape. What we see is a continuing fulfillment of our hope and of the assurance of the gradual illumination of the Earth consciousness as it evolves toward a more *sattvic* state. Progress, although shadowed by the still only partly transformed vital forces within human nature, gives us strong encouragement that the goal of a harmonious world can and will be won. I have selected only a small number out of many possible examples for discussion. [5-19]

One of the most luminous expressions of progress is *The Earth Charter* [5-20]. This document was initiated within the Assembly of the United Nations and presented at its environmental summit in Rio de Janeiro in 1992. In the spirit of the *U.N. Charter*, adopted in 1945, it sets forth broad integrated policies and principles for continued sustainable human existence on our planet in the face of unprecedented environmental degradation, poverty and conflict.

The Earth Charter is a plea and an exhortation to action arising from ecological awakening to our inescapable shared dependence on Earth's resources and to our sacred inner bond with one another and with our Earth-home. Although not yet formally adopted by the General Assembly, it is serving as a tool used at every level of education in dozens of nations throughout the world. Inspiring discussions of the Earth Charter's history, scope and place in the quest for a global ethical practice are available in Bird et al. (2016) [5-21] and Ferrero and Holland (2002) [5-22]

Closely tied to *The Earth Charter* are the *Millennium Development Goals* [5-23] adopted by the United Nations in 2014 and currently the subject of numerous international programs and services. Among the seventeen goals are the need to 1) eradicate extreme poverty and hunger; 2) achieve universal primary education; 3) promote gender equality and empower women; 4) reduce child mortality; 5) improve maternal health; 6) combat HIV/AIDS, malaria and other diseases; 7) ensure environmental stability; and 8) forge a global partnership for sustainable development.

In 2015, current Pope Francis I, having taken his name from St. Francis of Assisi (1182-1226), [5-24] issued a detailed Encyclical Letter entitled *Laudato Si' - On care for our Common Home.* Section 10 reads

I do not want to write this Encyclical without turning to that attractive and compelling figure, whose name I took as my guide and inspiration when I was elected Bishop of Rome. I believe that Saint Francis is the example par excellence of care of the vulnerable and of an integral ecology lived out joyfully and authentically. He is the patron saint of all who study and work in the area of ecology, and he is also much loved by non-Christians. He was particularly concerned for God's creation and for the poor and outcast. He loved and was deeply loved for his joy, his generous self-giving, his openhearted-ness. He was a mystic and a pilgrim who lived in simplicity and in wonderful harmony with God, with others, with nature and with himself. [5-25]

In the six chapters and 246 sections of *Laudato Si'*, Pope Francis integrates the ecological and scientific wisdom of the 21st century with the Church's social and moral teachings and draws not only Catholics but every person on the planet into a dialogue about our Earth-home. Chapter five is devoted to *"Lines of approach and action"*, stressing education, national and local policies, politics, economics, and dialogue between science and religions. Chapter six is a moving contemporary restatement and reemphasis of St. Francis' message eight centuries ago about the integration of environmental education with spirituality. The themes are truly universal, and in reading through the whole Encyclical, one could almost believe it written by an Indian sage, a Buddhist or an indigenous shamanic elder.

When I was an undergraduate at Amherst College in the early 1960s, I signed up to take a course in ecology, as an elective for my biology major. One of my professors advised me not to waste my time, because ecology was "for bird-watchers and elderly garden-ers". To be on the cutting-edge of science, the adviser said, I should be taking courses like genetics and biochemistry. Needless to say, times have changed in some areas of education. Sixty years ago, there were no majors in environmental studies, and the word "sustainabil-ity" was not yet connected to environment in dictionaries.

In elementary education, environmental themes are part of many curricula ranging from mathematics and science to language skills and social studies. Many public-school systems have established links with local city, state and national parks where elementary school children can be guaranteed at least a few visits to natural en-vironments. In my region of southeast Florida, there are regular field trips to Crandon Park (sandy beach and seagrass beds) and Fairchild Tropical Garden (one of the stellar tropical gardens in the Americas).

In his revelatory and controversial book, *The Great Work*, [5-26] geo-theologian [5-27] Thomas Berry draws our concern to the axis of higher education, economic policies, politics, and corporate disregard for the fabric and stability of the global environment. He views universities presently as partners in collusion with corporate and financial institutions educating students in business, science, and economics without providing any meaningful ethical professional foundation. He argues passionately for universities to reevaluate their largely abdicated position as cultural illuminators of the lower propensities of human nature, especially for those who will be directly involved in the scientific-commercial-financial-political sector and who may move into positions of leadership.

To use one of many possible examples of our disconnection from the processes of Nature, ecological studies of population dynamics clearly and unmistakably show that all populations in nature exist in balance with food, predators, weather conditions, disease and suitable habitat. If any of these limiting factors decreases in severity, the population will grow; if conditions become more severe, the population declines. The result is fluctuating numbers of organisms whose average over time gives a value for *carrying capacity*, or the number of individuals that an environment can support sustainably. No population of any species can sustain constant growth.

Earth and her resources are finite entities. Economics is grounded in functions of Earth resources and ecosystem services. The idea of "growth is good, and high rates of growth are even better" is at odds with our scientific understanding of ecosystem dynamics, with the spiritual basis of the planet and with common sense. Only in the last two or three decades has the discipline of *environmental economics* begun to challenge this widely perpetuated fallacy.

Although Berry (1915-2009) was a student of Eastern spirituality and culture, there is no evidence, judging from his publications, that he knew or read any of Sri Aurobindo's writings. Nonetheless, he would almost certainly have applauded Sri Aurobindo's analysis of the lower vital tendencies in humanity when he wrote (in 1917!)

Either knowledge must enlarge itself from above or be always in danger of submergence by the ignorant night from below. Still more must it be unsafe, if it allows enormous numbers of men to exist outside its pale uninformed by its light, full of the natural vigour of the barbarian, who may at any moment seize upon the weapons of the civilized without undergoing the intellectual transformation by their culture ... Knowledge must be aggressive, if it wishes to survive and perpetuate itself; to leave an extensive ignorance either below or around it, is to expose humanity to the perpetual danger of a barbaric relapse.

If science has thus prepared us for an age of wider and deeper culture ... it has encouraged more or less indirectly both by its attitude to life and its discoveries another kind of barbarism -- for it can be called by no other name -- that of the industrial, the commercial, the economic age which is now progressing to its culmination and its close.

This economic barbarism is essentially that of the vital man who mistakes the vital being for the self and accepts its satisfaction as the first aim of life ... To the natural unredeemed economic man beauty is a thing otiose or a nuisance, art and poetry a frivolity or an ostentation and a means of advertisement. His idea of civilization is comfort, his idea of morals social respectability, his idea of politics the encouragement of industry, the opening of markets, exploitation and trade following the flag, his idea of religion at best a pietistic formalism or the satisfaction of certain vitalistic emotions. He values education for its utility in fitting a man for success in a competitive or, it may be, a socialized industrial existence, science for the useful inventions and knowledge, the comforts, conveniences, machinery for production with which it arms him ... [5-28]

Sustainability & Stewardship

From the yogic perspective, it is the Creator who sustains His creation. This is so despite what humans may or may not do to be in harmony with the dynamics of the global environment. The Earth belongs to the Creator and not to the creation, although the two are inseparable, as the Promise of the Creator and the Hope of the creation are inseparable.

However, as our collective consciousness expands to reveal our spiritual relationship with our Earth-home, we set new and higher standards for our *dharma*. This new vision is producing such statements as *The Earth Charter* stressing sharing, accommodation for the well-being of one another and of the life of the planet. Our subservient sustaining role is linked to our evolution from a primarily *rajasic*, aggressive and possessive mode to one more *sattvic*, loving and self-giving.

Stewardship also needs clarification and a larger context. The common meaning of environmental stewardship is that humans are stewards either for God or for the generations of humans and other creatures yet to come. Clearly, we have not been doing a very good job. If God were given the pretend-role of a human "absent ruler", he would probably be shocked to see what we have done in his "absence". He might have second thoughts about his choice of stewards. If the absent beneficiary is future generations, they would also be appalled and terrified at our handiwork.

In the Judeo-Christian tradition, one of the most widely known and misinterpreted biblical pronouncements about the relationship of humans to the Earth is found in *Genesis 1: 26-30*.

Then, God said, 'Let us make man in our image; after our likeness; and let them have dominion over the fish of the sea, and over the birds of the air, and over the cattle and over every creeping thing that creeps upon the Earth. So God created man in his own image, in the image of God he created them; male and female he created them. And God blessed them, and God said to them, 'Be fruitful and multiply, and fill the Earth and subdue it; and have dominion over the fish of the sea and over the birds of the air and over every living thing that moves upon the Earth.' [5-29]

Lynn White [5-30] voiced what many feel about this passage, that it legitimizes the ruthless, destructive and even rapacious ethics held by many nations and their industrial corporations about the Earth's resources and biodiversity. However, recent new exegeses of this passage by David Goodin [5-31] reveal that it is more accurate to interpret the lines "have dominion" in terms of the compassionate and loving relationship that God has for his human children. We should use the same qualities in our spiritual relationship with Nature and the Earth, which Goodin terms *"a sacred accord with nature and all its biodiversity"*.

Goodin's insight brings both the God-human relationship and the bond between humans and Nature into focus. Aside from the philological merit of his work, his view is essentially the yogic perspective, since it implies that the binding force of Creator and the universal creation is one based on love and compassion. At this moment, in general, we may be terrible stewards, but there are bright signs that we recognize past mistakes and want to improve.

One very bright sign of our aspiration to improve our stewardship is intensifying as we speak. In 2018, a 15-year-old Swedish Girl, Greta Thunberg, took time off from school to begin a solo protest outside Swedish Parliament in Stockholm. She carried a hand-lettered banner announcing *School Strike for Climate*. As I write, she has sparked a global movement, fueled primarily by hundreds of thousands of young people, that has involved over 100 nations. She has addressed the United Nations and the World Economic Forum in Davos. Her movement's message is simply that the issue of climate change needs to be addressed... *Now*. The title of her new book [5-32] begs the question of what could happen if all of us plunged into radiant action on behalf of the Earth.

After all, we are in the process of evolution, under divine aegis. At some future point, the apotheosis of Nature will fulfill the Creator's Vision, and the Creator will fulfill the creation's aspiration and realization that He has kept in place since the beginning. Once we are awake, there is no reason why the process should proceed at a snail's pace. Once the hope is dynamically engaged, the Promise will increasingly make itself felt.

Medical *Dharma*:
Ayurvedic Science

The Vedas, transmitted from the creator Vishnu to the gods and thence to the yogis on Earth contains an entire volume on healing, the *Arthava Veda*. The *Vishnu Purana* again and again assures us that in the creation of the Earth all the provisions for inner and outer well-being were an integral part of divine dispensation. Like all Vedic wisdom, the healing herbs of the Earth are the property of all and available to all, a blessing of *prakriti*, the Divine Mother.

The highest texts and laws of healing are *shastra*, the verses of Vedic scripture. Ayurvedic physicians have the yogic goal, the *dharma* of being divine instruments of God, conduits for healing but not the doers themselves.

> *May Lord Purari (Shiva), in whose brilliance shines Bhavani (the Divine Mother, Parvati, Shiva's consort), just as wonderful herbs shine in the moonlight spread on the slopes of the Himalayas, grant us prosperity.*

> *Diseases arise for many reasons such as natural causes, external agents, internal agents, karma and others. To get rid of them and obtain happiness the physician should make use of efficacious recipes.*

> *Innumerable are the varieties of potent herbs which shine like gods; physicians should acquire infallible knowledge of their various properties.* [5-33]

Considering what we have explored in the previous chapters, if we first understand that our life is not confined to a single body for a very limited time, but is both a continuous universal and individual human experience, the latter of perhaps many past lives, then it follows that any system of medicine that seeks effectively to heal disease or imbalance in our life should of necessity address the furthest reach of our life's scope.

Second, if we are aware that Nature is not merely a complex collection of events, produced by purely material, physical forces, but a consciously guided progressive evolution playing out through the vehicles of the physical, vital, mental, and spiritual aspects of our existence, it becomes easier to suppose that Nature herself has always been providing the remedies for whatever ills, imbalances and disharmonies may have assailed us on our journey.

Third, if we go even farther to believe that karmic aspects of our past lives are in the process of resolution in our present life, then a healer will need to take into account the karmic origin of some of our disease in diagnosing and treating our health.

Finally, if we accept ourselves personally as an integral part of cosmic evolution in which our ultimate state will be a fully conscious and illumined union with our inner Source, then a healer will also have to assess and try to ameliorate our personal level of happiness and harmony with respect to that realization.

Ayurvedic medicine operates under the fundamental premise that our physical body is the outer representative of our being and subject to forces arising not only in our physical environment but also to the vital, mental and spiritual realms operating from within. Diagnoses are therefore more comprehensive and require methods and therapies that correspond to the source of the imbalances causing us suffering.

Students learning Ayurvedic healing have to learn the familiar aspects of medicine, e.g. internal medicine, anatomy, toxicology, pediatrics, surgery, psychiatry and geriatrics. They also treat many ailments that result from karma, and so they must learn Indian *jyotish* astrological practice to determine whether they should strive to cure the condition or only manage the symptoms. Vital and mental disorders require knowledge of the *chakras* and subtle nerves (*nadis*).

Ayurveda recognizes six stages of the manifestation of illness. Expressed in the language of Ayurvedic diagnosis they are:

- aggravation
- accumulation
- overflow
- relocation
- buildup in a new site
- clear physical manifestation of a recognizable disease

These stages describe imbalances in the three primary energies (*doshas*) of the body (*vata, pitta* and *kapha*) from their initial origin to the production of gross symptoms.

Most Western modern diagnostic technologies can detect only the final stages of disease, but Ayurveda detects the most subtle initial stages and can begin to restore balance through appropriate treatments. The methods used to restore balance are herbs, diet, aromas, gems, minerals (including mercury, gold, silver, and copper), colors, yoga (including meditation, *pranayama*-breathing exercises as well as hatha yoga postures), mantras, lifestyle and, as a last resort, surgery. Balance is restored by reducing factors or energies in excess and supplying or stimulating ones that are deficient. [5-34]

In the Ayurvedic *materia medica* are more than 2,000 plant species native to India and surrounding areas. With wider application to other regions of the world there are bound to be many more thousands of species that have potential use. Because Ayurveda arose from yogic meditative experience, ancient plant specialists were trained to concentrate and meditate on plants and were able to see exactly what therapeutic benefit each species had to offer. My own Ayurvedic physician recently expressed his sadness that one of the last trained plant diviners had passed away, and now no one (at least that he knew) could still perform this remarkable and valuable service.

In Ayurveda, a vegetarian diet is considered most healthy, but a few animal products are used, some quite widely. In India, cows are sacred animals because they symbolize the love and compassion of Mother Earth for all creatures including humanity. In the poetic symbolism of the Vedic hymns, cows represent inner and outer wealth and socio-spiritual status. Both butter and milk serve extensively in Ayurveda. *Ghee* (clarified butter) is both a food staple and a component of many medicines and is used as well as in their preparation from raw materials. Milk, also an Indian dietary item, is part of many treatments including the *panchakarma* therapy with which I have had personal experience. My personal physician has instructed me to take the daily herbal treatments he prescribed dissolved or suspended in warm milk. Milk and *ghee* can of course be obtained without harming the cow.

Ayurveda respects the more advanced consciousness of animals and, for karmic considerations, does not use products that would injure or kill the provider. Feathers, bone, dung, urine, musks, and other materials that are cast off by an animal, or that can be collected without injury, are used. But, in comparison to plant-based medicines, they are few in number.

Ayurvedic psychiatry, which includes all aspects of forces acting upon the mind, pays attention to visual stimuli, especially color. Color enters our system through the eyes and stimulates *prana* flowing to the mind, affecting the quality of thoughts and emotions we experience. Therapies may include changes in the type of lighting used in the home or office, colors of clothing worn and outdoor natural surroundings with the goal of promoting happy, progressive thoughts and feelings.

Swami Sada Shiva Tirtha, at the end of his detailed discussion of color therapy counsels us *"Nature's colors are the most beneficial, nourishing and strengthening."* [5-35] In light of all we have discussed about Nature, this should not be surprising, since Nature's colors have surrounded us since the beginning of creation. Perhaps one of the best things we can do if we feel sad, depressed, frustrated, or angry is to take a walk in a park or even look through a window at a natural landscape. This principle is at work in the widely practiced Nature

Therapy, Forest Bathing [5-36]. This has become a principal therapy in Japanese medicine, both in preventative care and healing.

Prior to the Industrial Revolution, nearly all medicines were derived from natural sources, primarily plants, including plants used as food (*e.g.* spices, cabbage, garlic, onions, and ginger), but also some from mineral and animal sources. This is not only true of all indigenous cultures but also for the nations of Europe and their colonies. Also, in Eastern cultures, particularly in India and China, natural medicines still form the mainstay of traditional practice although now augmented by contemporary pharmaceuticals, surgery, and diagnostic technologies.

With the rise of the petroleum, pharmaceutical, and chemical industries of North America and Europe in the late 19th and 20th centuries and the greatly increased wealth that accompanied them, production and use of natural medicines has declined sharply, and the consciousness of medical practice has changed dramatically.

Allopathy, the predominant medicine practiced in Western nations, is primarily the palliative treatment of symptoms and has only recently begun to address the root causes of disease and focus increasingly on prevention, something that is fundamental to Ayurveda. Partly because of the very high and escalating costs currently associated with pharmaceuticals, hospitalization, diagnostic technology and health insurance, many people are returning to proven and effective natural treatments, "alternative" therapies including herbal medicines, Ayurveda, homeopathy and Chinese traditional medicine, none of which has yet to fall completely within the grip of the commercial exploitation of corporate power.

Banned and nearly extirpated over several centuries of foreign occupation, Ayurvedic medicine has had a great revival since Indian independence in 1947. New hospitals, clinics and medical schools continue to flourish, and this aspect of Vedic wisdom is increasingly being sought and practiced worldwide.

I hope, as we discover our wider and deeper connections with universal Nature, a truth embedded in the spiritual foundations of Ayurveda, we will see a renaissance of natural healing. The character of this expanding renaissance will be the confluence of elements of this ancient Indian science with newer allopathic methods and with the vast resources of natural indigenous medicine from every part of the world. I hope too that as we recognize the inherent promise and value of every human soul, we shall provide medical care, the gift of Mother Earth, to all her children. The *dharma* of medicine is to assure treatment to those in need as a sacred right. Our slow and often painful journey toward illumination can yet embrace love, sympathy, kindness, respect and a deep understanding of what it means to be a human being.

Notes for Chapter 5

5-1.   Sri Chinmoy, 2015. *Victory to my Lord Supreme.* p. 103. Perfection-Glory Press, Augsburg, Germany.

5-2.   Sri Aurobindo. 1997. *Essays on the Gita.* pp. 171-172. Sri Aurobindo Ashram Press, Pondicherry, India.

5-3.   *The Vishnu Purana.* 2015. *trans.* by H.H. Wilson. Written by Rigvedic Maharishi Parashara.

5-4.   Manu can refer to the archetypal man, or the archetypal human dynasty or clan. In the *Vishnu Purana* it also designates the principal rulers of different successive periods (*manvantaras*) of human history.

5-5.   Pliske, Thomas E. 2017. *Light, Truth and Nature.* Chapter 6, *Our Environment*, pp. 143-183. Pacem in Terris Press, Washington, D.C.

5-6.   I have adapted this hierarchy from J.H. Withgott and S. Brennan. 2008. *Environmental Science*, 3rd ed. Similar arrangements are widespread in environmental science and ethics course materials and texts.

5-7.   Swimme, B.T. and M.E. Tucker. 2011. *Journey of the Universe. xi* + 175 pp. Yale Univ. Press, New Haven, CT. This book presents the latest scientific "creation story" of the universe from the initial "flaring forth" of the Big Bang to contemporary environmental crises. It has all the chemistry, astrophysics, molecular biology, ecology and evolutionary ideas of our age rolled into a tightly organized and highly accessible package. Swimme was a colleague of the late Thomas Berry, so there are many elements and ideas of Berry's *The Great Work* that pervade this fascinating book.

5-8.   *The First Estate* (Television show). 1984. Interview with Sri Chinmoy, Russell Barber, host. WNBC-TV (New York).

5-9.   Berry, Thomas. 2002. in Ferrero, E.M. and J. Holland, *The Earth Charter: A Study Book of Reflection and Action.* p. 17. Redwood Press.

5-10.   Louv, Richard. 2006. *Last Child in the Woods – Saving Our Children from Nature-Deficit Disorder. x* + 334 pp. Algonquin Press, Chapel Hill, NC. Louv's book has ignited a growing interest and support for environmental education. A school program begun in Washington State called *No Child Left Inside* has spread to many other US states and communities over the past decade. Although the programs are varied, all focus on outdoor activities and field trips to local natural areas.

5-11.   Carson, Rachel. 1962. *Silent Spring. xxvi* + 368 pp. Houghton Mifflin Co. Publ.

5-12.   Carr, Nicholas. 2011. *The Shallows – What the Internet is Doing to Our Brains. viii* + 280 pp. W.W. Norton and Co., NY.

5-13.   Wilson, E.O. 1984. *Biophilia.* pp. 1-2. Harvard University Press, Cambridge MA.

5-14.   Campbell, J. 2004. *Mythic Worlds, Modern Words.* pp. 3-8. New World Library, Novato CA. In this book, Campbell's primary task in the elucidation of the mythic symbolism used by James Joyce in his novels, *Portrait of the Artist as a Young Man, Ulysses,* and *Finnegan's Wake.* For those new to Campbell's understanding of myth and spirituality, the transcriptions of his many interviews with PBS commentator Bill Moyers in *The Power of Myth* (1991, Anchor Books, NY) is a good place to begin.

5-15.   Sri Aurobindo. 1973. *Sri Aurobindo and the Mother on Art, Part 1.* pp. 4-9. Originally published in *The Hour of God.* Sri Aurobindo Ashram Trust, Pondicherry, India.

5-16.   Ibid.

5-17.   Sri Chinmoy. 1974. *Yoga and the Spiritual Life.* p. 120. Agni Press, Jamaica, NY.

5-18. Sri Chinmoy. 1999. *Sri Chinmoy Answers, Part 17.* pp. 18-19. Agni Press, Jamaica, NY.

5-19.   Pliske, Thomas E. 2017. *Light, Truth and Nature, Chapter 6 – Our Environment.* pp. 143-183. Pacem in Terris Press, Washington, D.C.

5-20. The text is available at www.Earthcharter.org

5-21. Bird, F., S.B. Twiss, K.P. Pedersen, C.A. Miller and B. Grelle. 2016. *The Practice of Global Ethics.* Edinburgh Univ. Press. Edinburgh, Scotland, U.K. Chapter 2 is particularly relevant.

5-22. Ferrero, E.M. and Joe Holland. 2002. *The Earth Charter: A Study Book of Reflection and Action.* Redwood Press.

5-23. United Nations. 2014. *Millennium Development Goals Report 2014.* United Nations, NY.

5-24. The flavor of St. Francis' spiritual embrace of creation is best communicated through his *Canticle of the Creatures (Cantico delle Creature)*

5-25. Pope Francis I. 24 May 2015. *Encyclical Letter Laudato Si' – on the Care of our Common Home, Section 10.* Our Sunday Visitor Publishing Division, Huntington, IN.

5-26. Berry, Thomas. 1999. *The Great Work. xi* + 241 pp. Three Rivers Press, NY.

5-27. Berry coined this word to describe his personal focus on the immanence of the divine within the physical forms of universal Nature and the Earth.

5-28. Sri Aurobindo, 1994. *India's Rebirth,* 3rd ed. pp. 126-127. Originally published in the journal *Arya,* 1917. Institut de Recherches Evolutives, Paris.

5-29. *Holy Bible, Revised Standard Edition.* 1952. Thomas Nelson & Sons, NY. Genesis: 1:16-30. pp. 1-2

5-30. White Jr., Lynn. 1967. *The Historical Roots of our Ecological Crisis.* Science 155: 1203-1207.

5-31. Goodin, David M. 2005. *Understanding Humankind's Role in Creation: Alternate Exegeses on the Hebrew word 'Kabash' and the Command to Subdue the Earth.* in *Studies in Science and Technology* (SSTh). Vol. 10: *Streams of Wisdom? Science, Theology and Cultural Dynamics*: Lund, Sweden. Lund University Press. pp. 293-311.

5-32. Greta Thunberg. 2019. *No one is Too Small to Make a Difference.* 80 pp. Penguin Books.

5-33. *Sarngadhara-Samhita.* 14th century treatise on Ayurveda. 1.1, 1.4, 1.5, p. 3. K.R. Srikantha Murthy, trans. 2012. Charu Printers, Varanasi, India

5-34. Swami Sada Shiva Tirtha. 1998. *The Ayurvedic Encyclopedia,* Ayurveda Holistic Center Press, Bayville, NY. An accessible, detailed and indispensable source for anyone wanting to learn the history, principles and practice of Ayurvedic medicine.

5-35. Ibid. pp. 331-332.

5.36. Forest bathing is a Japanese and Ayurvedic therapy in which one simply walks, relaxes or meditates in a natural forest environment. Details are available in [Qing Li, Dr. 2018. *Forest Bathing.* 320 pp. Penguin Random House Publishers, New York.]

EPILOGUE

W hatever our spiritual beliefs, we have to begin by accepting and claiming this world (including ourselves!) *as it is now*, a work in progress. Put another way, if like the ancient Vedic *rishis* and their modern counterparts, Sri Chinmoy and Sri Aurobindo, we believe that there is a higher creative Force guiding cosmic evolution, we have reason also to believe that there is steady movement toward an ultimate perfection. Then, whatever imperfection exists, whether in the world or in ourselves, it is a temporary condition, however painful and discouraging in the moment. It is of such conviction and promise that hope takes deep root.

The seeker Arjuna lives in each of us at the spiritual core of our being. The message from the Vedic seers, ancient and modern, and from the *Bhagavad Gita* is to dive within, find our universal connection through whatever path we choose and to receive the guidance for our radiant actions as agents of self- and world-transformation.

The Pilgrims
of the Lord Supreme

We are the pilgrims of the Lord Supreme
on the path of Infinity.
At this time we have broken asunder
obstruction's door.
We have broken asunder the night
of tenebrous darkness, inconscience,
and the eternal, indomitable fear of death.
The Boat of the supernal Light's dawn
is beckoning us.
and the World-Pilot
of the hallowed bond of Love divine
is beckoning us.
The Liberator's Hands are drawing us
to the ocean of the great Unknown.
Having conquered the life-breath
of the Land of Immortality
and carrying aloft the Banner
of the Lord Supreme
We shall return —
We, the drops and flames
of Transformation-Light.[E-1]

Note for Epilogue

E-1.   Sri Chinmoy. 1972. *My Flute.* p. 74. Aum Publ., Jamaica, NY.

APPENDIX:

FURTHER READING & STUDY

T he following titles and websites are suggestions for more background on the topics covered in the text. Some are mentioned in chapter endnotes, and some are additional. I provide abbreviated citations, since most if not all are in print and can be found quickly by an online search.

A. SRI CHINMOY & SRI AUROBINDO

Sri Chinmoy.

1. *Meditation: Man-Perfection in God-Satisfaction.* 1989. Aum Publ.
2. *Summits of God-Life: Samadhi and Siddhi.* 1999. Aum Publ.
3. *Death and Reincarnation.* 1997. Aum Publ.
4. *Sport and Meditation.* 2013. The Golden Shore Verlag.
5. *Everest Aspiration.* 1978. Agni Press.
6. *The Body, Humanity's Fortress.* 1974. Agni Press.
7. *Yoga and the Spiritual Life.* 1974. Aum Publ.
8. *My life's Soul Journey* (daily meditations). 1995. Aum Publ.
9. *Kundalini, the Mother Power.* 1992. Aum Publ.
10. *My Flute* (poetry). 1998. Aum Publ.
11. *The Vedas, the Upanishads and the Bhagavad Gita.* 1997. Aum Publ.
12. *Beyond Within.* 1985. Aum Publ.
13. *Eastern Light for the Western Mind.* 1989. Aum Publ.
14. *Mother India's Lighthouse.* Agni Press.
15. *The Dance of the Cosmic Gods.* 1974. Agni Press.
16. *Science and Nature.* 1996. Agni Press.
17. *The Garland of Nation-Souls.* 1995. Health Communications, Inc.

18. *The Divine Hero: Winning in the Battlefield of Life.* 2002. Watkins
    Watkins Publ.
19. *Master and Disciple.* 1985. Aum Publ.
20. *Astrology, the Supernatural and the Beyond.* 1974. Aum Publ.
21. *The Source of Music.* 1999. Aum Publ.
22. *Mother India's Lighthouse.* 1973. Rudolf Steiner Publ.

Analysis:

Sumadhur. 2018. *Sri Chinmoy, Fully Realized Spiritual Master - His Life and Philosophy.* Sumadhur Publ.

Websites:

www.srichinmoylibrary.com
www.heart-light.com

Sri Aurobindo

(unless otherwise noted, all titles are published by the Sri Aurobindo Ashram, Pondicherry, India.)

1. *The Life Divine.* 1977.
2. *The Synthesis of Yoga.* 1971.
3. *Rebirth and Karma.* 1991. Lotus Light Publ.
4. *Essays on the Gita.* 1997.
5. *The Secret of the Veda.* 1998.
6. *Letters on Yoga, Vols. 1-2.* 1970.
7. *India's Rebirth.* 2003. Institut de Recherches Evolutives
8. *Social Evolution Towards the Ideal of Human Unity.* 1985

Website:

www.sriaurobindoashram.org

B. INDIAN SPIRITUALITY, CULTURE & PHILOSOPHY

1. *Talks with Ramana Maharshi.* 2001. Inner Directions Publ.
2. Swami Vivekananda. *The Yogas and Other Works.* 1953.
   Ramakrishna-Vivekananda Center Publ.

3. *The Gospel of Sri Ramakrishna.*1992. Ramakrishna-
Vivekananda Center Publ.
4. *The Mahabharata* (several abridged versions are available)
5. *The Ramayana* (" " " " ")
7. *The Vishnu Purana.*
8. Sri Yukteswar. *The Holy Scinece.* 1974. Self-Realization
Fellowship.
9. Paramahamsa Yogananda. *Autobiography of a Yogi.* 1995.
Self-Realization Fellowship.

C. OTHER EASTERN PERSPECTIVES.

1. *The Teachings of the Buddha.*
2. Kapleau, P. *To Cherish All Life.* 1981
3. Kapleau, P. *The Wheel of Life and Death.*
4. *The Tao te Ching.*

D. ETHICS, THEOLOGY & PHILOSOPHY

1. Plato, *The Republic.*
2. Bird et al. *The Practices of Global Ethics.* 2016. Edinburgh Univ. Press.
3. Holland, J. *Postmodern Ecological Spirituality.* 2017. Pacem in Terris
Press.
4. Berry, T. *The Great Work.* 1999. Three Rives Press
5. Teilhard de Chardin, P. *The Phenomenon of* Man. 1959. Perennial
Library, Harper & Row.
6. Teilhard de Chardin, P. *The Divine Milieu.* 1960. Harper Torch-
books.7. Teilhard de Chardin, P. *The Future of Man.* 1964. Harper
Torch-
books.
8. Pope Francis I. *Laudato Si, On Care for Our Common Home.* 2015.
Our Sunday Visitor Publ.
9. St. Francis of Assisi. *Cantico delle Creature.*
10. R.W. Emerson. *Nature.*
11. W. Whitman. *Leaves of Grass* (poetry)
12. Wallace, A.R. *The World of Life: A Manifestation of Creative Power,
Directive Mind and Ultimate Purpose.* 1914. Hard Press Publ.
13. *The Essential Goethe*, M. Bell, ed. 2016. Princeton Univ. Press.
14. J. Campbell, with Bill Moyers. 1988. *The Power of Myth.* Penguin

Books.

15. G. Sessions, ed. *Deep Ecology for the Twenty-First Century.* 1995. Shambhala Publ.

16. E. Ferrero and Holland, J. *The Earth Charter: A Study Book for Reflection and Action.* 2005. Redwood Press.

Website:

www.earthcharter.org.

E. SCIENCE & TECHNOLOGY

1. Darwin, C. *On the Origin of Species.*
2. Kuhn, T.S. *The Structure of Scientific Revolutions.* 1970. Univ. Of Chicago Press.
3. Wilson, E.O. *Letters to a Young Scientist.* 2014. Liveright Publ.
4. N. Carr. *The Shallows: What the internet is Doing to Our Brains.*
5. B. Swimme and M. Tucker. *Journey of the Universe.* 2011. Yale Univ. Press.
6. Wallace, A.R. *The Malay Archipelago.* 2008. Periplus Editions Publ.
7. Pliske, T.E. *Light, Truth and Nature.* 2017. Pacem in Terris Press.

F. ENVIRONMENT

1. W.R. Wright and D. Boorse. *Environmental Science,* 13th ed. 2016. Pearson Publ.
2. Louv, R. *Last Child in the Woods.* 2006. Algonquin Books.
3. Carson, R. *Silent Spring.* 1962. Houghton Mifflin Publ.
4. Thunberg, G. *No one is Too Small to Make a Difference.* 2019. Penguin Books.
5. Wilson, E.O. 1984. *Biophilia.* Harvard Univ. Press.
6. Wallace-Wells, D. *The Uninhabitable Earth: Life After Warming.* 2019. Jim Duggan Books.

Websites:

The Forum on Religion and Ecology at Yale has a wealth of information and contacts on the intersection of spirituality and environment with points of view East, West and Indigenous.

http://fore.yale.edu/information/index.html
www.ssgnetwork.org

G. AYURVEDIC & NATURAL MEDICINE

1. Swami Sada Shiva Tirtha. *The Ayurvedic Encyclopedia*. 1998. Holistic Center Press.
2. David Frawley. *Ayurvedic Astrology*. 2005. Motilal Banarsidass Publ.
3. Svoboda, R.E. *Ayurveda*. 2004. The Ayurvedic Press.
4. Li, Qing. *Forest Bathing*. 2018. Penguin Random House Publ.
5. S. Popham. *Evolutionary Herbalism*. 2019. North Atlantic Books.

H. INDIGENOUS PEOPLES

1. Chief Oren Lyons and Alexander Ewen. 1994. *Voices of Indigenous Peoples Address the United Nations*. Clear Light Publ.
2. Winona Laduke. *All Our Relations*. 1999. South End Press.
3. Winona Laduke. *Recovering the Sacred*. 2005. Haymarket Books.
4. K.D. Harrrison. *When Languages Die*. 2007. Oxford Univ. Press.
5. *United Nations Permanent Forum on Indigenous issues*. 28 July 2000. United Nations Economic and Social Council Publ. E2000/22
6. *United Nations Declaration on the Rights of Indigenous Peoples*. March, 2008, Publ. 07-586-81.

OTHER BOOKS

FROM PACEM IN TERRIS PRESS

RUINED FOR LIFE
Post-Missionary Immersion, Reintegration, & Conversion
David Masters, 2019

SEEKING GLOBAL JUSTICE & PEACE
Catholic-Inspired NGOs at the United Nations
Emeka Obiezu, 2019

ROMAN CATHOLIC CLERICALISM
Three Historical Stages in the Legislation of a Non-Evangelical,
Now Dysfunctional, and Sometimes Pathological Institution
Joe Holland, 2018

CATHOLIC PRACTICAL THEOLOGY
A Genealogy of the Methodological Turn to Praxis,
Historical Reality, & the Preferential Option for the Poor
Bob Pennington, 2018

SAINT JOHN OF THE CROSS
His Prophetic Mysticism in the Historical Context
of Sixteenth-Century Spain
Cristóbal Serrán-Pagán y Fuentes, 2018

BRETTON WOODS INSTITUTIONS & NEOLIBERALISM
Historical Critique of Policies, Structures, & Governance of the International Monetary Fund
& the World Bank, with Case Studies
Mark Wolff, 2018

THE WHOLE STORY:
The Wedding of Science & Religion
Norman Carroll, 2018

PADRE MIGUEL
A Memoir of My Catholic Missionary Experience in Bolivia
amidst Postcolonial Transformation of Church and State
Michael J. Gillgannon, 2018

POSTMODERN ECOLOGICAL SPIRITUALITY
Catholic-Christian Hope for the Dawn of a Postmodern Ecological Civilization Rising
from within the Spiritual Dark Night of Modern Industrial Civilization
Joe Holland, 2017

JOURNEYS TO RENEWED CONSECRATION
Religious Life after Fifty Years of Vatican II
Emeka Obiezu, OSA & John Szura, OSA, Editors, 2017

THE CRUEL ELEVENTH-CENTURY IMPOSITION OF
WESTERN CLERICAL CELIBACY
A Monastic-Inspired Attack on Catholic Episcopal & Clerical Families
Joe Holland, 2017

LIGHT, TRUTH, & NATURE
Practical Reflections on Vedic Wisdom & Heart-Centered Meditation
In Seeking a Spiritual Basis for Nature, Science, Evolution, & Ourselves
Thomas Pliske, 2017

THOMAS BERRY IN ITALY
Reflections on Spirituality & Sustainability
Elisabeth M. Ferrero, Editor, 2016

PETER MAURIN'S
ECOLOGICAL LAY NEW MONASTICISM
A Catholic Green Revolution Developing
Rural Ecovillages, Urban Houses of Hospitality,
& Eco-Universities for a New Civilization
Joe Holland, 2015

PROTECTION OF RELIGIOUS MINORITIES
A Symposium Organized by Pax Romana at the United Nations
and the United Nations Alliance of Civilizations
Dean Elizabeth F. Defeis & Peter F. O'Connor, Editors, 2015

BOTTOM ELEPHANTS
Catholic Sexual Ethics & Pastoral Practice in Africa:
The Challenge of Women Living within Patriarchy
& Threatened by HIV-Positive Husbands
Daniel Ude Asue, 2014

CATHOLIC LABOR PRIESTS
Five Giants in the United States Catholic Bishops Social Action Department
Volume I of US Labor Priests During the 20th Century
Patrick Sullivan, 2014

CATHOLIC SOCIAL TEACHING & UNIONS
IN CATHOLIC PRIMARY & SECONDARY SCHOOLS
The Clash between Theory & Practice within the United States
Walter "Bob" Baker, 2014

SPIRITUAL PATHS TO
A GLOBAL & ECOLOGICAL CIVILIZATION
Reading the Signs of the Times with Buddhists, Christians, & Muslims
John Raymaker & Gerald Grudzen, with Joe Holland, 2013

PACEM IN TERRIS
Its Continuing Relevance for the Twenty-First Century
(Papers from the 50th Anniversary Conference at the United Nations)
Josef Klee & Francis Dubois, Editors, 2013

PACEM IN TERRIS
Summary & Commentary for the Famous Encyclical Letter
of Pope John XXIII on World Peace
Joe Holland, 2012

100 YEARS OF CATHOLIC SOCIAL TEACHING
DEFENDING WORKERS & THEIR UNIONS
Summaries & Commentaries for Five Landmark Papal Encyclicals
Joe Holland, 2012

HUMANITY'S AFRICAN ROOTS
Remembering the Ancestors' Wisdom
Joe Holland, 2012

THE "POISONED SPRING" OF ECONOMIC LIBERTARIANISM
Menger, Mises, Hayek, Rothbard: A Critique from
Catholic Social Teaching of the Austrian School of Economics
Pax Romana / Cmica-usa
Angus Sibley, 2011

BEYOND THE DEATH PENALTY
The Development in Catholic Social Teaching
Florida Council of Catholic Scholarship
D. Michael McCarron & Joe Holland, Editors, 2007

THE NEW DIALOGUE OF CIVILIZATIONS
A Contribution from Pax Romana
International Catholic Movement for Intellectual & Cultural Affairs
Pax Romana / Cmica-usa
Roza Pati & Joe Holland, Editors, 2002

Books from Pacem in Terris Press,

are available for purchase from Amazon at:

amazon.com

amazon.uk

amazon.de

amazon.fr

amazon.co.jp

amazon.es

amazon.it

www.ingramcontent.com/pod-product-compliance
Lightning Source LLC
Chambersburg PA
CBHW060927040426

42445CB00011B/822